# Praise for UNQUENCHABLE

The wealth of wisdom that pours forth in every page of *Unquench-able* is staggering. For bruised believers who are wondering how to withstand the harsh realities of life, Carol Kent's insights and encouragements will be a soothing balm to the soul. Each chapter will tend and revitalize the fire of your faith until it is a raging blaze that cannot be extinguished.

PRISCILLA SHIRER, speaker
and author of *The Resolution for Women*

Carol's unwavering, unquenchable commitment to our Father has been an example to me about what it means to live with courageous faith. The theme of her book reminds me of Isaiah 64 — that God would come down and, as fire sets brushwood ablaze and causes water to boil, make his name known. The God who acts on behalf of those who wait for him is able to meet your needs too.

KAY ARTHUR, Bible teacher,
founder of Precept Ministries, and author

Carol Kent is a woman of faith who is familiar with disappointment, disaster, and even despair. In *Unquenchable*, you will also discover she is a friend who will walk with you through the fires of your life, offering clear compassion and substantial hope. Read this book for yourself and then pass it on to someone who also needs to know they, too, can survive the furnace.

ELISA MORGAN, speaker, author of *The Beauty of Broken*,
and publisher of *FullFill* magazine

Once again my friend Carol Kent has written a book that will forever leave an imprint on my heart. I wept as I read much of it, tears acknowledging the pain of life and tears of deep gratitude at the redemptive mercy of our God, who catches every one of those tears.

SHEILA WALSH, Women of Faith speaker
and author of *The Storm Inside*

A consummate storyteller, Carol Kent introduces us to Jackie, Lynn, Cindy, Ace, Carrie, and others who show us what a loving God can accomplish, even in the most challenging situations. Carol also shares her own honest struggles, teaching us how to fan the dying embers of our faith into a bright and burning passion for God.

LIZ CURTIS HIGGS, bestselling author
of *The Girl's Still Got It*

If you long for an unquenchable faith that not only survives difficult times but thrives in the midst of them, this book is for you! With honest and tender vulnerability, Carol Kent provides the tools we need to reignite our faith, opening our hearts once again to the incredible and unquenchable love of God.

JOANNA WEAVER, author of *Having a Mary Heart
in a Martha World*

Imagine your worst nightmare comes true — your health is in jeopardy, your child runs away, your job is history, your faith is a mystery. Now what? With sensitivity and insight, Carol Kent unwraps the reasons we go on and reveals how we can add fuel to our spiritual fire and develop an unquenchable faith.

PATSY CLAIRMONT, Women of Faith speaker
and author of *Twirl: A Fresh Spin at Life*

Carol Kent embodies the definition of unquenchable. She unveils her own life, bringing us into the corners and crannies of her heart where we find wisdom won in painful places. She paints a picture of a God who is bigger than our sorrows and more powerful than our pain.

JENNIFER KENNEDY DEAN, executive Director of
The Praying Life Foundation and author of *Live a Praying Life*

*Unquenchable* is the kindling, the propellant, the bellows of hope fanning the embers of faith until your life becomes a wildfire of intimacy with the all-knowing, all-loving, all-powerful, always-there-for-you God. Carol and Gene Kent's unquenchable faith will fortify your own as you see the footprints to follow to get out of your pain and into the promise of God's love and power.

> PAM FARREL, bestselling author of many books, including
> *Men Are Like Waffles, Women Are Like Spaghetti*

*Unquenchable* is a masterfully woven mosaic of faith that catches fire, and those flames keep faith's embers aglow. I continue to be challenged and transformed by Carol Kent's personal faith journey and by the stunning stories she shares of the unquenchable fire in the lives of fellow faith sojourners. This is a book to cherish and hold near.

> GARI MEACHAM, president of Truly Fed Ministries and
> author of *Watershed Moments*

Our choices in this life affect the quality of our journey toward heaven. If anyone knows about pain and choices, it is Carol Kent. She has chosen well — she has chosen God. *Unquenchable* reflects all she says and does, and it causes the flicker of the flame of God's life in each of us to be set ablaze.

> KATHY TROCCOLI, recording artist, author,
> and director of Among Friends events

Carol, God has given you a gift. Thank you for the sacrifices you made to write this book. You are an inspiration of redeeming the time with your books and with your speaking engagements. You have brought genuine hope, helping others to develop a faith in God that is unquenchable, no matter what the firestorm.

> FERN NICHOLS, founder and president
> of Moms in Prayer International

With a deeply compassionate heart, Carol Kent communicates profound biblical truths in a way that creates a hunger for more of the Jesus she loves. A thought-provoking story of God's deep love and supernatural provision, *Unquenchable* is a compelling read that will inspire and challenge anyone who wants to experience God's transforming power in their life.

ALLISON BOTTKE, bestselling author of
the award-winning Setting Boundaries® book series

Thanks, Carol, for your willingness to be transparent and allow God to use you in ways you hadn't imagined. You've increased my desire for an all-out wildfire faith!

DR. BEV HISLOP, professor of pastoral care at Western
Seminary and author of *Shepherding Women in Pain*

If you've ever doubted God or wondered if his Word and promises are true, this book is for you. With incredible honesty, Carol Kent shares more of her journey through the flames of pain and disappointment, and what she continues to learn as God refines her faith. This inspiring book teaches the biblical truth of living with an eternal perspective, pointing the way to facing the fires of our lives with unquenchable faith.

MARY WHELCHEL, director of women's ministries
at The Moody Church, Chicago

If you are looking for a book that will help you lead a small group on a journey to discovering a faith that burns with passion, no matter what challenges life brings, this is it. The "Come to the Fire" section at the end of each chapter provides questions that will become the springboard to discussions that draw your group into a transformational experience.

LESLIE VERNICK, licensed counselor and bestselling
author of *The Emotionally Destructive Relationship*

I love all of Carol Kent's books, but *Unquenchable* just might be the best yet. Carol's honesty and transparency will challenge you to seek until you find this kind of wildfire faith that comes through the trenches of suffering. The stories will help you understand God's plan to use our earthly suffering for our ultimate good and for his glory.

CAROLE LEWIS, national director of First Place 4 Health
and author of *Live Life Right Here, Right Now*

Has someone or something put your fire out? Are you feeling your life doesn't matter or you have no purpose? Then read *Unquenchable*! Carol Kent shares openly from her experiences and from the Scriptures how God can place a fire in you that will not go out and will spread to those around you. It warmed our hearts and rekindled the fire in our lives, and it will do the same for you!

PHIL AND DEBBIE WALDREP,
Phil Waldrep Ministries, Decatur, Alabama

*Unquenchable* set my soul ablaze to grab hold of faith in a new and audacious way. Carol Kent is a breathtaking storyteller who writes each word with a pure and honest love for others to know God more deeply through their own faith journey. God's Word saturates the book and points to the one promise that should drive us all: No matter what happens in life, our God remains faithful to us.

KASEY VAN NORMAN, bestselling author
of *Named by God* and *Raw Faith*, kaseyvannorman.org

If you need to know that God is real even when life screams otherwise, this book is for you. Carol Kent has an unquenchable faith that cannot be extinguished. She will teach you how to recover your faith and hold on to Jesus.

ARLENE PELLICANE, author
of *31 Days to Becoming a Happy Wife*

True wildfire faith means having strength, endurance, and a solid, abiding trust in God — in darkness and light, in pain and wellness, in sadness and laughter. Carol Kent reminds us that no matter where we are or what our circumstances may be, because we are the image bearers of Jesus Christ, the ground we're standing on is holy ground.

DR. TIM CLINTON, president of American Association
of Christian Counselors

We've all been there. Shattered dreams. Unfulfilled longings. Disappointment with God. Times when life seems to toss us overboard without a twig to cling to. Carol Kent understands — she's been there and back. In *Unquenchable*, Carol encourages us not to lose hope and gently shows us how to endure, thrive, and once again have a wildfire faith that will take our breath away.

SHARON JAYNES, conference speaker and author
of *Praying for Your Husband from Head to Toe*

Is the reality of your life different from what you hoped it would be? Do raging storms of tragedy threaten to douse the flickering flames of your once-strong faith? Someone understands. Carol Kent and countless others have walked treacherous paths through fiery furnaces and have chosen refinement rather than ashes. *Unquenchable* is full of real stories. Real pain. Real hope. Reading it may just spark a wildfire in your own faith journey. And you will never be the same.

LUCINDA SECREST McDOWELL, author and speaker,
EncouragingWords.net

Fire is a powerful and fascinating picture of spiritual truths. Carol Kent's gift of masterful writing and storytelling touched my heart with captivating illustrations of God's unquenchable work. A fabulous read!

CANDY DAVISON,
Sandy Cove women's ministry coordinator

# UNQUENCHABLE

## GROW *a* WILDFIRE FAITH
## *that* WILL ENDURE ANYTHING

# CAROL KENT

ZONDERVAN

*Unquenchable*
Copyright © 2014 by Carol Kent

This title is also available as a Zondervan ebook. Visit www.zondervan.com/ebooks.

Requests for information should be addressed to:

Zondervan, *Grand Rapids, Michigan 49530*

Library of Congress Cataloging-in-Publication Data

Kent, Carol, 1947-
    Unquenchable : Unquenchable : grow a wildfire faith that will endure
anything / Carol Kent.
      pages  cm
    Includes bibliographical references.
    ISBN 978-0-310-33099-8 (softcover) 1. Christian life. 2. Spiritual
formation. I. Title.
    BV4501.3.K463 2014
    248.4—dc23                       2013034146

14 15 16 17 18 19 20 /DCI/ 20 19 18 17 16 15 14 13 12 11 10 9 8 7 6 5 4 3 2 1

*To my remarkable sister,*
*Paula Afman —*
*your brave decision to choose unquenchable faith*
*amid unthinkable circumstances*
*renews my hope and makes my spirit soar.*
*I love you.*

# Contents

# CHAPTER 1

# When the Fire Goes Out

When circumstances seem impossible,
when all signs of grace in you seem at their lowest ebb,...
when love and joy seem well-nigh extinguished in your
heart, then cling ... to God's faithfulness.

**David Tryon, "But How?"**

A growing sense of hopelessness was casting a long shadow over my faith. Did God even care about us? I wasn't sure which was more frightening — the reality of the life-threatening accident I'd just had and the resulting financial challenges I was facing, or the fact that my faith, always vibrant and unshaken until then, was suddenly struggling for survival.

I was twenty-two years old and had been married about six months. My husband and I had moved to Grand Rapids, Michigan, where Gene was taking some graduate classes and I was working as an administrative assistant for furniture maker Steelcase.

One day the accelerator pedal on my car stuck as I was approaching a red light on my way to work in rush-hour traffic.

I pressed hard on the brake pedal, but my car picked up speed. Swerving into an open lane, I was unable to guide my fast-moving vehicle into a complete right-hand turn, and I hit the car that was waiting to make a left-hand turn. That car hit the vehicle behind it.

Not stopping upon impact, my car careened down the street. I glanced at the gas gauge. It was half full. I knew I could not run the car out of gas before probably causing a terrible accident in the next intersection. I pulled on the emergency brake, which slowed the car down just a bit. In a desperate attempt to stop, I steered the automobile toward a telephone pole, opened my door, and — with my heart hammering — jumped from the car, landing and rolling on the hard pavement, expecting the car to hit the telephone pole. But it didn't!

My now driverless car hit the curb, missed the pole, and went right into the next intersection and hit another car, which then hit the car behind it. (If you're counting, you know this was now a five-car collision.) I jumped up from the ground, amazingly with no more than a few abrasions, and watched in horror as my car turned in a circle in the intersection, jumped the corner curb and dislodged a fire hydrant, turned in another circle in the intersection, and destroyed a park bench. After one more circle, it crashed into the plate-glass window of the IBM building and finally came to a stop.

Out of all the drivers involved, only two women sustained minor injuries, and no one was seriously hurt. We were grateful there was no loss of life. But the property damage was extensive. We assumed our auto insurance would cover us, until the day after this horrible accident when we discovered we had *no* insurance. When we left the Christian organization my husband and I worked for previously, they "gifted" us with six months of additional auto insurance. But because of a clerical mistake, we were, in fact, totally uninsured.

Gene and I barely had enough money to put food on the table each week and were still trying to pay off our student loans, so we knew we were in deep trouble. To make matters worse, the day after we made the second large payment to our attorney (with borrowed money), the local newspaper ran an article on him. It read, in part: "This man has been disbarred from practicing law in the state of Michigan because of indecent exposure in his office." We had prayed for God's help following the accident. How could God let this happen?

We were financially ruined, emotionally exhausted, and spiritually devastated. Didn't God love us? Rather than feeling loved by an omnipotent God, for the first time in my life I felt abandoned by him. My sense of spiritual passion wavered as I mentally listed the ways Gene and I felt we had been let down — first by the mechanical malfunction, then by the office worker who made such a major clerical error with our insurance, and finally upon discovering that the statute of limitations in Michigan allowed cases involving this accident to be brought to court for up to seven years. I wrestled with soul-searching questions:

➔ Why would God allow this to happen? Gene and I had considered the possibility of teaching missionary children at an academy in Brazil, but I wasn't allowed to leave the United States until pending lawsuits were resolved.

➔ Why did God allow us — a young Christian couple — to experience a financial wipeout that left us uncertain for up to seven years, not knowing if we would be able to pay all our bills and build a secure future?

❧ Why didn't my miracle-working God fix that stuck accelerator pedal before it caused so much damage? Did he like to do miracles only when there was a crowd watching?

❧ If God chose not to protect people like us who were eager to serve him, why should we trust him in the future?

I tried to read my Bible and pray, but it was painful to turn to the God who was supposed to take care of me but hadn't. Where was he? I had given him my heart as a young child and passionately pursued him throughout my university years and as a newly married woman. But now I didn't even feel like talking to him. I was mystified and hurt that God would allow such bad things to happen to us. The result? A spiritual numbness settled into my soul. The fire of my faith, it seemed at the time, had been doused by a flood of doubts and despair.

That was over thirty years ago. If I could whisper into the ear of the young woman I was, I would say, "Don't despair. Your faith won't fail. Just the opposite. It will grow even stronger through this trial."

What I wouldn't tell myself, but what is also true, is this: "I know you think this is a major tragedy, but believe me, this is *nothing* compared to the tragedies you will know in your life!" Thankfully, God, in his wisdom, knows better than to tell us what trials lie ahead. One day's worries are enough for us to bear.

I'd love to tell you that once my faith survived that trial it never again wavered. But that wouldn't be true. In fact, the flame of my faith has, at times, dimmed to the point that all I had were a few flickering embers in a bed of cold, gray ashes.

I know I am not alone in that experience. Perhaps you've reached the same point yourself. My friend Jackie knows it well.

## A Fire Grown Cold

From the first time I met her, Jackie has been a source of spiritual encouragement to me. We met when our paths crossed at a conference where we were both speaking, and I was moved by her fiery passion for God and her desire to do his work in creative ways.

Whenever I'm with Jackie, she sparks my desire to do more with my spiritual gifts to accomplish God's goals in this world. An African-American woman committed to racial reconciliation, Jackie makes me more aware of the importance of encouraging Jesus lovers from many denominations and cultures to join forces as we pursue his calling. She allows God to use her to bring people groups together for his kingdom purposes.

Jackie's example has motivated me — not just once but multiple times over a period of years. I always look forward to her encouraging notes on Facebook and to the times she shows up in an audience where I am speaking. From the platform, I connect with Jackie's eyes and she nods in acknowledgment. Her unspoken words are translated to my heart as, "You *go*, girl! God is going to do remarkable things at this conference. I'm here praying for you, and I can hardly wait to see how he will move!"

I think of Jackie as a Christian with unshakable faith — a woman with deep spiritual roots that give her stability and strength for whatever happens in her life and ministry. She once told me that her faith began to grow as a child when she watched her mom pray for food when there was nothing left in the cupboard to feed Jackie and her five siblings. Before the prayer was even finished, someone knocked on the door and dropped off several bags of groceries. Jackie said, "We asked for bread, and the floodgates opened. It was easy for me to view God as a provider."

This early experience fueled her faith. As time moved on, Jackie believed God would provide jobs and other daily needs, and she saw him answer prayers. Life wasn't perfect, but she knew the truth of Proverbs 20:24 — her steps were directed by the Lord, and that truth gave her confident expectations about the future.

Then, not long ago, I received a surprising e-mail message from Jackie:

> In the last two years, my faith has come to a crisis. My life seems to have lost its luster. My interest in participating in church activities has waned. My loving husband longs to bring a light back into my eyes. The smallest things cause me to stare into space and weep, wishing for days gone by when there was fire in my faith, enthusiasm in my voice, and hope in my heart.

I wondered what brought about this extreme change in my friend's outlook. Her e-mail continued:

> On September 28, my precious mother called in the morning, as she always did, so we could pray together. She told me she hadn't been able to breathe well during the night and didn't think she was going to make it. I prayed with Mom hurriedly and made arrangements to get her to the hospital. Even though I was two hundred miles away, I was able to arrive in time to speak to her one more time. On October 1, she went home to be with Jesus.

Jackie and her siblings carried on in pain as they made plans to care for their father, who had just lost the love of his life after sixty-five years of marriage. She described "the press of grief" weighing on her and her siblings. The hardest moment each day was in the morning when Jackie had usually prayed over the phone with her mother, but now she wasn't there to talk to.

Then her sister was diagnosed with breast cancer and began chemo treatments. The following July, Jackie's sixty-one-year-old brother had a massive heart attack, and once more the family came together to walk slowly behind a casket to say good-bye to a loved one. Jackie wrote, "It was heart-wrenching to see my father bury his youngest son. I was sure God would provide grace and comfort, but the pain was unbearable." She went on to share further news:

*Then Dad began to weaken, making the risk of falling so great that he couldn't be left alone. He grew weaker each day, went to sleep on January 5, 2013, and woke up in heaven.*

As I read Jackie's e-mail, I realized that these multiple losses, so close together, rocked her faith. The words that followed stunned me.

*I'm spent. I'm moving on autopilot. My spiritual fire is dim. The embers are smoldering. I know after all of his suffering Job said, "I know that my redeemer lives ..." I still believe he lives, but it's easier to type those words than to truly experience feelings of faith and hope.*

Jackie's letter ended with questions.

*What has happened to my once rock-solid faith?*

*When will I see this sorrow bringing glory to God?*

*When will I have the energy and desire to serve God with the vibrancy I once had?*

I love Jackie's questions. Instead of giving superficial answers to gut-wrenching cries of the heart, she dared to ask the questions we are often afraid to acknowledge. I respected her honesty as she described the numbness that comes when there has been so much sadness and loss that we no longer have the ability to function normally. Her honesty gave me permission to admit that I, too, know what it feels like to have my spiritual flames extinguished by disappointment in God when he could have orchestrated a more favorable outcome.

As I travel the world and meet with Christians in every walk of life, I listen to many who are suffering with unfulfilled hopes and unmet longings. Many of us have experienced disappointment in a God we know is powerful enough to have stopped our pain — but didn't. We've known the power of a time when our fire burned brightly and warmed our hearts and recharged our dreams — but no more. The fire has dwindled low. God's Word doesn't speak to us. We can't spur ourselves on to verbalize a prayer. We question God's love. We feel spiritually dead.

Have you felt this way?

Perhaps you, like me, can identify with author Philip Yancey, who wrote, "True atheists do not, I presume, feel disappointed in God. They expect nothing and they receive nothing. But those who commit their lives to God, no matter what, instinctively expect something in return. Are those expectations wrong?"

## A Discouraged Prophet

Our experiences of disappointment and questioning God are not unique to modern times. The prophet Elijah experienced this same crisis of faith. It had been fifty years since Israel occupied the pinnacle of power under David and Solomon. There was tremendous corruption in the land, and it was in a state of religious, moral, and social rot. God's chosen spokesperson for this hour of darkness was Elijah. He experienced extraordinary high points as the most famous and dramatic of Israel's prophets. He predicted the beginning and end of a three-year drought, and he was used by God to restore a dead child to his mother. Then in a dramatic scene on Mount Carmel, he represented God in a showdown with priests of Baal and Asherah — and God won big-time! But times of great spiritual victory are no guarantee against times of deep spiritual lows.

The day after the big victory on Mount Carmel, King Ahab told Jezebel everything Elijah had done and how he killed all the false prophets. And this powerful woman, furious at Elijah's success over the prophets of her people, announced that she planned to have him killed.

God had just done astonishing miracles in Elijah's life and ministry, and now a single, angry woman was coming after him. Do you know what he did? He ran for his life! He was so afraid that when he came to Beersheba in Judah, he left his servant there and went another day's journey into the desert. He came to a broom tree, sat down under it, and prayed to die: "'I have had enough, LORD,' he said. 'Take my life; I am no better than my ancestors'" (1 Kings 19:4 NIV). Talk about feeling like the fire of your faith burned out — this was it! This man was beyond discouraged; he was so depressed he longed for death.

## What Causes Our Faith to Wane?

How about you? Do you sometimes wrestle with disappointment with God, deep discouragement, or diminished trust in God's faithfulness?

Each one of us has our own trigger points for what wears us down to the point of feeling like the fire of our faith is going out. For some, it might be great personal loss or a series of losses; for others, it might be the burnout of working hard in business or ministry without visible results or much-needed breaks. Many people experience a spiritual indifference that develops over time when the busyness of everyday demands dulls their spiritual fervor. It can come from self-imposed isolation or from too much pressure to succeed. Doubts and unanswered questions about why God allows certain events — when tragedy befalls good people while evil seems to prosper — sometimes leave us discouraged or feeling betrayed, wondering if our faith makes any difference at all.

One look at the notes I've received over the past few months confirms how universal this struggle is.

**Cathy:** Sometimes indifference sneaks in to extinguish my spiritual fervor, and I find it very difficult to restart spiritual disciplines once I stop.

**Heather:** Massive changes have been taking place in my church where I was employed full-time in women's ministries. I am worn-out, angry, and hurt. I'm even ticked off at God for allowing this to happen. There is a distance between God and me that I haven't experienced before.

**Julie:** My sister and I are twins. She just gave birth to her second baby, and during this same time period I've had three miscarriages. I've prayed and begged God for a child, but he isn't answering my prayer — and it feels so unfair. I love my sister, but every time I see her holding her infant, I feel a cold shiver of faith-shaking fear that I will never have a baby of my own. It makes me question God's love.

**A single missionary:** I've ministered in a remote South American location for over forty years, where I've experienced extreme hardships as well as heart-stopping spiritual victories. Now I'm approaching retirement, and the mission I'm with is going under financially. After promising to provide a modest retirement for me, they've just told me there are no funds available once I leave my field of service. I feel alone and abandoned. As if the God I served all of these years has forgotten me. I still know he's my Savior, but I am confused by his lack of provision for my future. I feel disappointed in him.

These are all women who pointed others to hope, faith, and truth, but the spiritual fervor they once experienced is faltering amid the challenges they are experiencing. My heart aches for the ruins of the relationship they once had with God.

For me, the fire grew cold when I became disappointed in God because he did not stop my son from taking the life of another man. If you don't know that story, I'll fill you in briefly in the next chapter. But even without knowing the facts, I imagine you can understand that because I believed God is all-powerful and all-knowing, I knew he was aware of the horrific events unfolding. Yet he still allowed my son to choose death and destruction. The result was the worst ash heap of our lives — inconsolable grief for the family members of the deceased, severe pain for multiple members of our family, a lifetime of prison for our son, and the excruciating reality for

Gene and me that our treasured son had committed murder. Surely a loving God would have used his almighty power to change this life-altering, dream-smashing, faith-rocking, death-producing event.

Whatever the cause, it seems as if, sooner or later, many of us find ourselves in the ash heap of a spiritual fire that has gone out.

## Is There a Remedy?

Why do some people weather such firestorms with their faith intact, able to heal and grow, while others become bitter, turn from God, and find themselves unwilling or unable to ever believe in God again? Why do some cling to or return to faith but merely limp along, while others soar in new boldness and strength? These are questions we all ask. Perhaps the reason we feel so much fear when our faith falters is that we are afraid we will be left with nothing but a cold ash heap.

Having been on the ash heap and back to a vibrant, bold faith, I have found myself longing to find a way to encourage others not to lose hope, but instead to endure, to thrive, and to once again burn with a wildfire faith that takes our breath away.

I've walked through enough life to know better than to offer simple checklists and shallow action steps to transform a waning faith back into a roaring wildfire faith. There are no easy answers to such penetrating questions. But there *are* truths we can cling to, practices we can turn to, stories we can draw strength from, and God's mercy that we can fall on. There is hope and help.

This book is my invitation to you to join me on a journey of discovering these truths, choosing these practices, and falling into the strong arms of the God who is the author and finisher of our faith. In the following pages we will explore true stories — stories from Scripture, my own life, and the lives of others I've known — of those who have endured hardship and whose confidence in God has been worn down, perhaps even reduced to ashes, but whose faith has been rekindled and has come out stronger than ever before.

Elijah's experience at his lowest point offers a hopeful example. While fleeing for his life, the food and drink he needed were provided by an angel — a supernatural experience. I can attest that at my lowest point I did *not* experience that kind of divine intervention. What I *did* experience, however, was more akin to what unfolded next for Elijah. Following a forty-day journey, he finally heard from the Lord, though not in the expected, supernatural ways. God did not appear to him spectacularly through the wind or in the earthquake or in the fire. God came to him in a whisper and provided him with encouragement, comfort, and a plan of action. God's gentle whisper blew on the dying embers of the faith of a man who was burned out emotionally and spiritually, and he was eventually able to move forward. It took time and patience, but the flame of his faith did once again burn brightly.

That gives me hope that the same can be true for each of us!

## The Journey

My friend Lynn can relate to that experience. I met Lynn through a group of fellow authors and speakers. It didn't take long for me to recognize her spiritual insight, which quickly captured my heart. We kept in touch over the years and often prayed for each other as we faced challenging circumstances. Recently Lynn wrote to me about a huge struggle she was going through in her faith journey. Here's the story in her own words:

As I sat silently across the table from my beloved octogenarian friend—who is as mature in spiritual stature as in years—I had difficulty absorbing what Jillian was saying as she struggled to express her distance from God. I had never heard her talk this way before in the twenty-some-odd years I had known her. She was, in my eyes, a spiritual giant and a glowing example of faith to whom I looked for godly counsel. Surely, after all these years of faithfulness, she could not be growing cold toward God. I had always thought her faith was unquenchable.

Her shocking words described the deafening silence and deepening darkness of her spiritual life that I, too, was experiencing, but which I found too painful to articulate. Like Jillian, I could no longer hear from God.

I longed for Jillian to throw a lifeline of wisdom I could clutch to pull myself from this apathetic void. Instead, it seemed that we were both swirling hopelessly into a godless maelstrom. Listening to her only exacerbated my own angst. I had known times of desperation, times of feeling out of touch with God, even times of feeling his discipline, but this was different. I couldn't feel his presence at all. I was stone-cold.

Shaken by the discovery that Jillian and I were suffering the same distance from God, I decided to listen attentively over the next few weeks to other women I encountered. I found these same tendrils of distance and despair winding through our conversations, revealing how many of us felt our intimacy with God was being sucked from us.

The unsettling truth is that these women were once strong, mature Christians who had been intimate with God—filled with his joy, fueled by his purpose, serving him with abandon. Now they were distant, emotionless, and deadened to the voice of God.

And I was one of them.

How had I succumbed to this passionless state?

Lynn's no-holds-barred description of the downward spiritual progression of women who once had a vibrant faith in God rang true to me. She went on to describe her own experience with a long series of deep personal losses, especially the death of her father. Then she offered an insight:

My heart had frozen shut in what poet Emily Dickinson described as "the Hour of Lead"—a chilling stupor that wraps the heart in catatonic armor to shield it from unimaginable grief. But sadly, I had also allowed this frigidity to shield me from God's love and compassion. During the several years since my losses, I had only been reading the Bible haphazardly, and I'd stopped journaling my prayers with any consistency. This was tantamount to short-circuiting my communication with God. I was no longer petitioning him, praising him, or confessing to him. My spiritual fervor dissipated as a result. I now realized that every time I didn't pen a prayer of gratitude, confession, or praise, another layer of callus had been forming around my lifeless heart. Finally, apathy had taken over.

As I read Lynn's experience, I recognized similarities to Jackie's. Both of these women described the cold absence of God when heartache overwhelmed them. Both also mentioned their departure from the rhythm of walking with and talking to God that often accompanies our disappointment in what he has allowed to happen. Read how Lynn eventually addressed this distance:

Now God was unexpectedly using my talk with Jillian to pierce my frozen armor. For the first time in months, I picked up an old journal and began rereading the past passionate outpourings of my soul to the Lord. As I read he used the warmth of my own words to woo me back to him, and I began to long for the intimate relationship he and I had once enjoyed.

I began to write, begging God for a way back to him. He used my own pen like the strike of a match to ignite the flame. I couldn't stop writing. I started with the words, "Oh God, I don't even know how to pray anymore. I don't feel you. God, please get me back to you!" Graciously, God used this gift of written prayer to draw me back into his presence in a palpable way. Somehow the act of writing itself elicited feelings I didn't even know existed, feelings that had lain buried and dormant.

Over the next weeks, God used his Word in my daily Bible reading and my own words through journaling to breathe his Spirit on the flickering embers of my heart. God reminded me that I needed spiritual revival through daily confession and repentance. I was discovering that sin, perhaps more than any single thing, had ossified my heart and left me stone-cold toward God. A. W. Tozer wisely admonished, "Do a thorough job of repenting. Hasty repentance means a shallow spiritual experience. Let godly sorrow do her healing work. It is our wretched habit of tolerating sin that keeps us in our half-dead condition." I was already experiencing this to be true as I confessed my sin of apathy to God.

Lynn's journey reminded me of David, the psalmist, someone who also wrote out his prayers to God — his confessions, questions, failings, and honest thoughts. David learned that forgiveness brings true happiness and that it's only when we ask God to forgive our sins that he gives us real joy and relief from the burden of our separation from him. David's repentant heart is revealed in these lines: "Finally, I confessed all my sins to you and stopped trying to hide my guilt. I said to myself, 'I will confess my rebellion to the LORD.' And you forgave me! All my guilt is gone" (Psalm 32:5 NLT).

Lynn realized she needed additional spiritual practices to feed the newly flickering flame of her faith. She continued:

Isolation can be a devastating symptom of spiritual hardheartedness, and it only makes one's heart grow colder. In a state of indifference, we often cut ourselves off from fellow Christians and in so doing we extricate ourselves from the very sources necessary to ignite and sustain the fire of revival. As King Solomon wrote, "Two are better than one, because ... if either of them falls down, one can help the other up. But pity anyone who falls and has no one to help them up" (Ecclesiastes 4:9 – 10 NIV). In community, we learn we are not alone, because not only do others demonstrate genuine care; they have also experienced like circumstances, and from this we take hope.

So, with some trepidation but with a fervor lit by God, I invited the very women who felt far away from God to join me for a journaling class to pursue the Lord unreservedly, seeking personal revival. I had no idea if anyone would show up. But, surprisingly, a number of the women said they, too, longed for deep soul-searching that would probe and pierce their hearts and let God do his deep, redemptive work. They were willing for their pens to become God's blowtorch to ignite their passion.

At this point in my friend's story, God began convicting my own heart. Throughout the past thirteen years of my son's arrest, trial, conviction, sentencing, and life behind bars, there have been many times when I felt my heart toward God cooling. Lynn's words instantly prompted me to acknowledge that my natural tendency was to withdraw from being vulnerable with friends about the shakiness of my faith as I endured the lifetime prison sentence of my son. It felt too unspiritual to admit my doubts and fears — especially since I'm a Christian leader who makes her living speaking about a God of hope, redemption, and love.

Lynn went on to tell me about bringing together women who were willing to "come clean with God" about the frigidity of their faith. What she described gave me pause, along with the conviction of my sin of pride — not wanting to share my disbelief, disappointment, and heartache with others. Why? Did I believe people would think less of me for being honest? Did I believe they expected me to be a stronger Christian than I was? Did I think ministry opportunities would dry up if I admitted my humanness while continuing to live in a dark, hopeless situation? Was I too afraid to admit that sometimes I hated going to visit my son in such a detestable place? Lynn's soul-searching experience with her group impacted me deeply:

What transpired is nothing short of miraculous. We wrote vividly descriptive prayers of confession and prayers of lament, using the freewheeling self-expression of the psalmists. Psalm 62 underscores this idea of pouring out our hearts to God. The result? We realized all the more, after such cathartic release, that God alone is our refuge.

We pushed ourselves to answer probing questions posed by the psalmists such as, "Why are you cast down, O my soul?" "Why have you forgotten me?" "Why must I go about mourning, oppressed by the enemy?" We recognized that in the past, our lack of gut-wrenching honesty with God had prevented our revival. Now we journaled feverishly, no-holds-barred.

While wrestling with God in the passionate embrace of prayer, we drew closer to him, and our hearts warmed as they beat near his. So we wrote to complete a simple sentence: "Lord, I feel . . ." in order to encourage the expression of the full range of our emotions. With every stroke of our pens, we were becoming warmer toward the Lord.

After many weeks together, we knew it wasn't enough to confess our sins; we had to turn from them from that time forward. Deeply humbled, we penned prayers of absolute surrender to God and offered ourselves as living sacrifices to him, to live crucified lives, dead to sin and alive to Christ. We yielded our full selves at any price to obedience to his will for our lives. It was a fearsome step to be sure, but it was like pouring pure fuel on the heart-fires God had ignited. Fully surrendered hearts, lying unrestricted on the altar of personal sacrifice, are finally able to burn freely.

A few months passed, and when I met again with my friend Jillian, my heart was bursting to invite her to receive the same gift I had received. So I invited Jillian to pick up her own pen, cry out to God, make her confessions, and plead with him to help her write her way back to spiritual health, true fellowship, and passionate intimacy. I had no doubt that, if she were willing, God would revive and ignite her spirit just as he had mine.

Lynn described the immense transformations that many in her group experienced, such as years of bitterness melting into forgiveness and intense anger giving way to deep joy. These women had been set free from depression, doubts, and icy stoicism by the warm breath of God's Spirit through their willingness to communicate openly with God, to express their emotions freely, to name and abandon their sins, and to commit to live a crucified life. Their faith had once again become unquenchable!

## Daring to Be Honest with God

Jackie, Lynn, and I all agree that God is real, and regardless of feelings of alienation from him and even of disappointment and questions about what he has allowed to happen, *his Word is still truth*. Philip Yancey expresses it well: "Faith means believing in advance what will only make sense in reverse." To me that means there will be times when I feel like my faith is dying (or already dead), but if I hang on to whatever I have left of the faith that once burned in my heart and seek out God's presence, the phoenix will eventually rise out of the ashes of my dashed hopes, my discouraged heart, my isolation and numbness

But that rarely happens overnight. As Jackie said, "I know that my redeemer lives, but I'm not feelin' it right now." As I look back, I can see that I discovered once before — when I was that twenty-two-year-old, financially devastated newlywed — that the rekindling of my faith is a process of communication with God. I never got to the point of losing all faith in God, but I faced unanswerable questions about what faith looks like when life is hard. The struggle was intense for several months, and eventually that struggle became a compartmentalized fear when for the first time in my life I doubted the goodness of God. With that came the erosion of what had been a strong faith.

One day, a year into this journey, I dared to be honest with Gene and voiced my doubts about God out loud for the first time. It was freeing to admit that I felt God had been unfair to us and that he didn't seem to be answering our prayers or intervening on our behalf. And Gene admitted to feeling the same. Following a gut-wrenching talk about our deep spiritual drought, we got on our knees beside a chair in the kitchen. Together we told God how disappointed we were in him. I voiced my doubts about his love and spoke of my anger about what appeared to be unjust treatment. I said, "God, it is so unfair for us to be in financial limbo for seven years." Gene and I knew everything we owned could be taken away with just one lawsuit. I poured out my sorrow over the lawyer who had taken our money unethically.

It didn't happen overnight, but by choosing to talk to God honestly about my disappointment, anger, and other negative emotions, I drew closer to him. Eventually I came to the place of saying, "God, I humble myself before you, and I will quit trying to control the outcome of this accident." That decision led to a surrender that enabled me to begin trusting him again — an important lesson for me to learn. Just as Jackie and her friends realized the need for total surrender to God, even in the midst of their feelings of distance from him, I needed to surrender to him and trust even without answers to my questions.

Once surrendered, I was able to list the unexpected blessings that came as a *result* of the accident. Take a look at five of those blessings to see how my perspective changed from one of loss to one of blessing:

1. There were two legal cases brought against me, but in both instances I was declared "not guilty" and therefore not liable for damages because the accident was caused by a mechanical problem. We still had huge legal bills, but we were not fined for extensive damages.

2. I started to identify with people who had doubts about their faith. I was, for the first time, truly able to *listen* to them instead of giving pat answers to their hard questions about the goodness of God.

3. My life experience was deepened as I felt the pangs of living in a fallen world that is saturated with disappointments and unfulfilled expectations. It brought me to a place of practicing the discipline of moving forward by faith, not by sight (circumstances).

4. I learned to talk out loud about my doubts, and because I started doing it with my husband, that paved the way for us to continue providing a safe place for each other when we faced hard situations in the future.

5. I discovered that doubt and disappointment in God during our driest spiritual times can pave the way to a wildfire faith that in turn leads to an eternal perspective.

Author Nancy Guthrie writes, "Submission to God's sovereignty means bowing the knee whether or not we understand, whether or not we have it figured out, whether or not we agree. In that submission, we find the strength and the grace to keep going. We even find joy in the journey."

OK, I admit I don't "feel the joy" every day, but I am newly committed to a deeper level of honesty — and I truly desire to find the strength to burn brightly, even in desperate times. I want to follow through with this directive from the apostle Paul: "Don't burn out; keep yourselves fueled and aflame. Be alert servants of the Master, cheerfully expectant. Don't quit in hard times; pray all the harder" (Romans 12:11 – 12).

I long for that level of "rekindling" Lynn described, and I am choosing to begin where her friends did, by finishing this sentence: "Lord, I feel ..." For me, filling in that blank is painful. Because of my son's arrest, conviction, and lifetime prison sentence for a serious crime, my own life has unfolded far differently than I anticipated. If you were to open the pages of my journal, this is the prayer you'd read:

> *Lord, I feel hurt because I was a young woman with a*
> *heart for you. I wanted nothing more than everything you*
> *had for my future. I followed you with passion, energy,*
> *dedication, commitment, abandon, and enthusiasm. I*
> *wanted to change the world in any way you could use*
> *me — except in this way, through my son's incarceration.*
> *That is just too personal. Too hard. Too cruel. Right now,*
> *I long for a different way to grow spiritually and for a new*
> *adventure in faith that doesn't involve my son living in a*
> *disgustingly hard place. But in the middle of my ashes, I*
> *ask for your forgiveness for my sin of pride. I want an easier*
> *life, but more than that, I long to have my heart for you*
> *ablaze once again with the joy of my salvation and with*
> *the vibrancy of a well-fueled fire.*

It was a hard prayer to write, but it was also a healing prayer, one that helped me to surrender the burden of questions I could not carry alone. And in the surrender, I began to feel the warmth of connection with God that I had not felt for a long time.

## God of the Flame

What is the state of your faith today? Are you enjoying the first flame of faith and want to know how to keep that flame growing? Is your faith ablaze with bright flames so that those who surround you are drawn to its radiance and warmed by its heat? Are you a raging bonfire, your love for God burning so brightly that you are consumed by its passion and championing God in this dark world? Perhaps your fire has been burning for many years and you are like red-hot coals in the very heart of God's fire, igniting others and keeping them burning brightly. If your faith is at such a high point, join me in this journey to discover how to tend and fuel that fire to keep it vibrant and strong.

Or has your passion cooled, your light dimmed, your fire quenched? Are you trying desperately to keep a small flicker going? Or do you feel lost in a heap of cold ashes, wondering if you will ever again know the warmth of God's presence? If so, I invite you on this journey to feel the warmth of the Holy Spirit breathing new life on the embers of your faith and to experience the wonder of new flames bursting forth to pierce the cold darkness pressing down on you.

Our God is the God of the flame. Throughout history, God has chosen fire to represent his awesome power, his judgment and wrath, his protection, and his *shekinah* glory. He is the God who placed the flaming sword to guard Eden and who appeared to Moses in the burning bush and the pillar of fire. He is the God who protected his servants Shadrach, Meshach, and Abednego in the fiery furnace, who appeared to Elijah in the chariot of fire, who burst forth in flames on the altar, and who shines through the flaming eyes of the Son of Man on the throne. These are only a few of the images God has seared onto the pages of Scripture, that we might know him more fully.

God is the source of that first flicker that sparked your faith, and one day you will stand in his holy presence, look into the flaming eyes of Jesus, and see his burning love for you. But between that first flicker and that heavenly meeting, there is life to be lived on this earth. The challenge we all face is that life can dim our fire or even quench it, whether by the soggy mist of the mundane or the quenching downpour of crisis.

Now is the time to discover how to nurture God's fire in our lives into a wildfire faith. What is a wildfire faith? A wildfire, by definition, differs from other fires by virtue of its uncontrollable nature, massive size, the speed at which it spreads, its tendency to rapidly change direction, and its ability to leap over roads, rivers, and firebreaks. The intense heat and convection winds it produces can actually change weather conditions or even produce its own weather system, including violent tornados that send embers flying well ahead of the main fire front. These factors make wildfires notoriously difficult to extinguish.

Imagine having a faith with those same qualities — a faith so powerful, so massive, that it spreads uncontrollably and leaps over boundaries that try to contain or extinguish it. Such faith has the power not only to rise above the circumstances but also to change the "weather conditions" of our lives. Wildfire faith replicates itself, throwing sparks and embers far beyond its own boundaries, creating additional fires of faith that then spread in new directions.

Wildfire faith springs from God's Word and burns itself into your own story. It reveals the true power of the fire God has placed in you, fans the flames of your faith, stirs your passion, and emboldens you to spark new fires that will spread and forever change the landscape of this world.

Such a faith does far more than simply hold on when life tries to extinguish it. It leaps in new directions, finds new fuel to keep burning, turns up the heat of a cold and deadened heart — and is unstoppable!

I need *that* kind of faith. When life threatens to extinguish my faith, I need a wildfire faith that can endure anything. And I've discovered that we *can* experience a wildfire faith that will endure anything! I am thrilled you have joined me in the adventure to live a life of faith that is unquenchable.

## COME TO THE FIRE

At the end of each chapter, you are invited to "Come to the Fire," where you can pause and consider the implications and applications of the truths we've explored. The goal of this book is not for you to be a spectator of the wildfire faith of others, but to discover how to nurture the flame of your own faith by fueling and tending it until it, too, is an unquenchable wildfire.

1. Using the continuum below, what number best describes your faith right now?

| 1 | 2 | 3 | 4 | 5 | 6 | 7 | 8 | 9 | 10 |
|---|---|---|---|---|---|---|---|---|---|
| Cold ashes | | | Glowing embers, but not a raging fire | | | | | | Wildfire faith |

2. What factors/experiences have contributed to where you are in your faith at this time?
3. Elijah experienced extraordinary high points in his ministry and in his relationship with God, but he still

became discouraged and fearful when confronted with trouble. We all have our own trigger points for what wears us down to the point of feeling like the fire of our faith is going out. What kinds of events or experiences tend to cause your faith to waver or diminish?

4. Carol, Jackie, and Lynn share stories of a once-vibrant faith that cooled for a variety of reasons. Which of these women do you most identify with at this point in your life? Explain.

5. Carol prayed, *"Lord, I want an easier life, but more than that, I long to have my heart for you ablaze once again with the joy of my salvation and with the vibrancy of a well-fueled fire."* Beyond a change in your circumstances, what is the "more than that" you long for from God?

## FIRE-BUILDING CHALLENGE

Sometimes the best place to start growing your faith is by writing honestly about the condition of your heart — whether it is vibrant with faith, dry and lacking, or even in crisis. As you begin reading this book, take the time to write a note to God about where you are in your walk with him right now. Honestly express your doubts, questions, and fears. Or if you are in a faith-filled place in your life, express thanks to him.

# CHAPTER 2

# The Firestorm

That which appears to us to be limitation can
actually become our unexpected advantage and asset.
As we're forced to our knees once again,
we discover the holy and wonder-full gift of life.
Tim Hansel, *You Gotta Keep Dancin'*

Tragedy. Loss. *Crisis.*

These are certainly not the only experiences that cause the fire of our faith to wane. In fact, while for some a crisis may ignite disappointment with God that drains away faith, for others the challenge of a crisis can actually be the catalyst that stokes a faint faith back into a raging bonfire. No matter what our response to crisis, we can be sure it has a profound effect on our faith. Crisis tends to rip away all the secondary factors of our lives and leave us desperately clinging to what matters most.

For this reason, I've come to appreciate the term *firestorm* for a crisis, because it helps me remember that our God is not only the maker of flame but is intensely present and powerfully at work in the midst of any storm we encounter, often mysteriously so.

A firestorm is a continuous, intense, uncontrollable blaze characterized by extremely high temperatures and destructively violent winds. The central column of rising heated air creates a massive updraft that draws in surface air from all directions. This updraft continuously feeds the fire, often creating tornado-like whirls. *Encyclopædia Britannica* states, "Such a fire is beyond human intervention and subsides only upon the consumption of everything combustible in the locality." Does that definition aptly describe your crisis — continuous, intense, uncontrollable, destructive, violent, massive, tornado-like, beyond human intervention, all-consuming? It does mine!

## My Firestorm

If you have followed my story, you know my son, a U.S. Naval Academy graduate, was convicted of the first-degree murder of his wife's first husband. Believing he was saving his two stepdaughters from potential abuse at the hands of their father, Jason did the unthinkable.*

From the time of his arrest in 1999 through his conviction in 2002, I wondered if I could keep breathing and go on with life. I had been a Christian for years, but I struggled with how to put one foot in front of the other. Fears for my son's safety ate away at me. When I was in a church lobby or in the grocery story, I wondered if people knew my secret — that my son was a murderer. I went over and over in my mind what I could have done differently as a mother to prevent this terrible

---

* For the whole story, see my previous books, *When I Lay My Isaac Down* and *Between a Rock and a Grace Place*.

crime from happening. After two and a half years and seven postponements of his trial, the gavel came down, and the judge sentenced Jason to life in prison without parole.

Jason's arrest and eventual conviction started the worst firestorm of my life. I knew Jesus, but I began to wonder if I could trust him. I had many questions: Did God know the true heart of my son? Did he understand Jason's fears for his stepdaughters? Why didn't God stop this terrible thing from happening? Didn't he hear my daily prayers for my son from the time he was in my womb, praying for him to come to an early faith in Christ and asking God to use him in a powerful way for eternal purposes? Did all of those prayers mean nothing? Couldn't God have allowed the sentence to have an eventual end date instead of life without the possibility of parole?

Apart from the initial news of his arrest, Jason's sentencing was the most devastating time of my life. Journalists put cameras and microphones in our faces, hoping to get their story, and they loved zooming in on the weeping mama. It was an excruciating invasion of privacy at a time when I agonized for my son, wondering if the severity of his sentence would tempt him to take his own life. As he was put back in handcuffs and a waist chain before leaving the courtroom, he looked in my direction. I mouthed, "I love you, son." He mouthed back, "I love you too." We left the courthouse, and I was consumed with grief. I wondered if anyone had ever died of a broken heart. My breathing was labored, and my tears were uncontrollable.

In every direction I turned, I was battered by violent winds of despair and hopelessness that sucked the air from my lungs and intensified the heat of my suffering. My efforts to stop this fire through frantic legal maneuvering, begging God for mercy, and rallying prayer support from others seemed futile. A man was murdered — and my son pulled the trigger. To this day, I still ask God, *Why?*

"One day you'll wake up and discover you can breathe again. This agonizing pain will not be this acute for the rest of your life," a friend told me. She was trying to comfort me, to somehow convey that pain has a season when it is so intense that you doubt you'll be able to go on living. She explained that the mind and body eventually adjust to the reality of a new kind of normal, and life gets more tolerable. She added, "People learn to laugh again, and they become functional, even happy." Her years of counseling combined with our long friendship earned her the right to give me this encouragement. However, at that moment, when Jason had just been sentenced to life in prison, I didn't want what felt like false comfort. I just wanted to be alone with my pain.

## So What Has Happened Recently?

Years have passed since that first shocking month after Jason's arrest in 1999, and I admit my counselor friend was speaking truth to my heart, even though my mind wasn't ready to absorb it. By 2004, I had healed to the point that I wrote a book about my experience titled *When I Lay My Isaac Down*. Countless people have written during the past decade with their questions: Did Jason get an appeal? Is there any chance he will ever walk in freedom?

Many readers have prayed for our family as we live out a story far different from what we anticipated. I say thank you to those of you who are still standing in the gap through your powerful intercession.

Well-meaning people come up to me after speaking engagements and say, "God has told me your son will win his trial."

With emotions rising — reminding me I still have more healing to do — I want to yell, "Didn't you hear what I said in my message? The trial is over! Jason *did not* win his trial. According to Florida state law, he will be in prison until he dies." But I don't say it. I only think it. At several events where I've spoken during the past few years, people whispered in my ear, "The Lord has revealed to me that your son will be released very soon."

At one recent event, the senior pastor of a large church stood on the platform and proclaimed, "I never say things like this, but God is telling me, '*This* will be the year Jason Kent is released.' Believe with me! Say it out loud with me." Before long the entire congregation began to chant, "This will be the year Jason Kent is released!" The well-known pastor prayed with Gene and me with an authority and confidence that touched me to the soul.

How I wanted to believe it! How I longed for the day when I could pick up my son at the prison, feed him his favorite meal, and help launch him into a productive, purposeful life outside the razor wire. But the year came and went. And Jason is still incarcerated with the same sentence he had on the day his court case ended in April 2002.

As I've grown in my faith, I've learned most people sincerely desire the best for Gene and me and for our son. They long for a positive resolution that would return Jason to a life of freedom, with a chance to redeem past choices and have a fresh start. They care deeply and would never deliberately cause us hurt, so we forgive them quickly. If we did not forgive them, life would become a permanent disappointment. But these experiences remind me that we are still in the fire. I'm learning that some fires last a lifetime, and sometimes my passion for Jesus is red-hot, and sometimes it falters.

## The Miraculous Rescue

I love the book of Daniel. If you've ever wished God would come right out and reveal himself, boosting your own faith and striking awe in the hearts of people who don't yet know him, check out this book. It reveals that kind of drama.

Daniel wrote this book to the people of Judah to remind them of God's ultimate control over events. To understand this story, we need to know what was happening in the world at the time it was written. The Babylonian Empire had replaced Assyria as the world's superpower. Nebuchadnezzar's Babylonian army had conquered Judah, taking thousands of God's people to Babylon. Others had fled to Egypt, and Jerusalem and the temple had been looted and burned.

Let's zoom in on just one part of this unusual story. Some astrologers came to the king and reminded him that he had issued a decree: everyone who heard the sound of the musical instruments had to fall down and worship the image of gold, and whoever refused to do so would be thrown into a fiery furnace. Then these men turned in the names of Shadrach, Meshach, and Abednego, saying they paid no attention to the king and didn't worship the image of gold.

The king was furious with rage and summoned the men without delay. He told them if the accusations were true, they would be thrown into a blazing furnace. Their response was immediate:

Shadrach, Meshach, and Abednego answered King Nebuchadnezzar, "Your threat means nothing to us. If you throw us in the fire, the God we serve can rescue us from your roaring furnace and anything else you might cook up, O king. But even if he doesn't, it wouldn't make a bit of difference, O king. We still wouldn't serve your gods or worship the gold statue you set up."

DANIEL 3:16–18

The king was livid. He ordered that the furnace be heated seven times hotter than usual and commanded the strongest soldiers in his army to tie up the three men and throw them into the blazing furnace. The men were fully dressed, and as they were thrown in, the fire was so hot that it killed the soldiers who tossed them into the furnace.

King Nebuchadnezzar was watching, and he leaped to his feet and said, "Didn't we throw three men, bound hand and foot, into the fire?" (verse 24). The men told him that was correct. "'But look!' he said. 'I see four men, walking around freely in the fire, completely unharmed! And the fourth man looks like a son of the gods!'" (verse 25).

The rest of the story is history. The king called the men to come out, and all the people marveled because their bodies, clothing, and hair didn't even have the smell of fire on them. The king said, "Blessed be to the God of Shadrach, Meshach, and Abednego! He sent his angel and rescued his servants who trusted in him! They ignored the king's orders and laid their bodies on the line rather than serve or worship any god but their own." Then he said something I need to remember: "There has never been a god who can pull off a rescue like this" (verses 28–29).

Can you hear the awe in the words of that king? Do you believe you are loved by this same God? I want to have the kind of courage in my own firestorms that Shadrach, Meshach, and

Abednego had at the mouth of the fiery furnace. Their story gives us three important truths to remember as we face our own firestorms.

1. *Our God is the God who rescues.* But he rescues within his time frame and not our own. We may never know his reasons, but sometimes he rescues us *before* the fire and sometimes he rescues us *in* the fire. In my case, I hoped for God to rescue my son before he was thrown into prison, but through the prison experience God has nevertheless rescued Jason, Gene, and me from despair, and he has set our eyes on our eternal rescue.

2. *Our God is the God of the flame.* Satan is not God's cosmic equal. He does not have the power to create or control our firestorms. No matter how high the heat, we can trust that God is sovereign. This truth is what gave Shadrach, Meshach, and Abednego the courage to stand fast. It can do the same for us.

3. *Our God is with us in the fire.* God may choose not to "save" us from personally devastating circumstances, but he is as much at home in the fire as he is outside of it. We may suffer its heat and be battered by its winds, but God's eternal protection of us is secure. Whether we remain in the fire or are delivered from it, we can say what the king said: "There has never been a god who can pull off a rescue like this." In my son's case, the rescue has not been in delivering Jason from prison; it has been the powerful presence of "the fourth man" in the fire, who is walking with him in the firestorm of prison.

# The Years Following the Conviction

Following Jason's trial and sentencing, we went through all the steps involved in appealing at both the state and the federal levels, to no avail. It was a long, expensive, discouraging process. We realized — as we still do — that a life was taken, and there is rightfully a heavy price to be paid. And some would say the only justice is for Jason to spend the remainder of his life in prison.

But how we longed for some kind of hope that Jason would one day walk in freedom.

## A Sign of Hope

Then a most unexpected e-mail arrived in August 2006 from an influential person in a governmental position in Florida. He had read my book *When I Lay My Isaac Down*, and the note read, "I feel strongly that your son should make application for his case to be heard in front of the Florida Clemency Board in December." A burst of unexpected hope exploded in my heart. I thought, "Someone in a position of leadership in the state of Florida believes Jason is not a threat to society, and he doesn't need to be locked up for the rest of his life." At that moment I believed God not only heard my prayers but was in the process of providing the path to an eventual positive resolution.

My mind was spinning as I recalled the many people we had met over the past couple of years, influential people in and out of Florida government positions, who were able to connect us to others who could offer advice and tangible help. Gene and I often looked at each other and exclaimed, "Now, *that* was a divine appointment!" It happened repeatedly, and I wondered if our perseverance had finally paid off. Was God at work on a new kind of miracle?

After responding to the Florida official and expressing doubt that clemency could be an option, this response came: "Many people don't understand that clemency doesn't always mean instant release of an inmate. The clemency process can result in a commutation of a sentence, which means setting an end-of-sentence date. In your son's case, with a conviction of first-degree murder, you would definitely not be looking at instant release. The most you could hope for would be to receive an eventual end-of-sentence date."

My hope soared. Since Jason committed his crime when he was in his mid-twenties, even if his sentence was commuted to twenty-five or thirty years, he would still walk in freedom in this lifetime if granted some sort of clemency. Gene and I had more questions than answers, but we formed a plan of action.

It usually takes three to five years for clemency paperwork to make it to the top of the pile of thousands of applications from other inmates who request that their cases be evaluated by the Florida Parole Commission, the group that recommends a hearing before the clemency board. But we hoped we could get his case fast-tracked.

Then we had to take specific steps, all within the next four months. We needed people who believed Jason would not be a threat to society if he were ever released to sign petitions. We had to locate a minimum of three people of influence, particularly those in government, to write a personal letter to the governor and to the clemency board asking that Jason's case be fast-tracked. We had to file certified paperwork on Jason's case from the clerk of the circuit and county courts with his application for clemency. We needed people who knew Jason before and after his arrest to write letters of support for him to the clemency board, and then we had to deliver them. The letters had to voice confidence in his character and include the assurance that Jason had a strong network of family and friends who would assist him upon release.

The assignment was daunting — too time intensive for our busy ministry travel schedule — but that wasn't going to stop us. With much prayer and high energy, we began the clemency process — one e-mail, one phone call, and one letter at a time. As a mom, I wished Jason did not have to be informed; I worried about getting his hopes up, only to have his dreams toppled into ruins. But his full participation was, of course, necessary.

### The Marathon

We devoted every spare minute to the dream of getting Jason's case heard at the December clemency hearing. Like the men who lowered their needy friend on a mat through a roof to Jesus (Mark 2:1 – 12), our "stretcher bearers" — the remarkable group of family members and friends who prayed for us and provided tangible encouragement to us through the months and years leading up to the trial — once again supported us with intensive prayer and by writing letters. Radio stations heard about our need for signed petitions and put the word out on the airwaves. And the mail started rolling in. Hundreds of people signed petitions, and almost one hundred letters came from government officials, Jason's fellow Naval Academy graduates, teachers, pastors, family members, and others who had connections with Jason during every stage of his growing-up years, as well as from people who had gotten to know him during his years of incarceration. With hopes rising, I could feel the presence of the fourth man in the fiery furnace. I believed God was preparing the way for a miracle.

## The Phone Call

We continued waiting — until the day a call came from the governor's office. The caller identified herself as legal counsel to then Governor Jeb Bush. She was polite, but firm. "I have discussed your request with the governor, and Jason's case will not be fast-tracked because he is not desperately ill and has not been incarcerated for a prolonged period of time." My mind whirred as my heart sank, and I had trouble speaking. Before hanging up, she said, "Your son's case will be in the system, and it will eventually rise to the top, but of course that will be under another administration because Governor Bush will be leaving office at the end of December." Her voice softened, empathizing with our pain, and she continued. "Jason Kent has the best advocates any inmate could ever ask for. You have a wonderful family." And she hung up.

I felt ill. The disappointment was bitter. I wept uncontrollably.

## News from the Florida Parole Commission

Months passed. Jeb Bush left office, and Charlie Crist became our new governor in the state of Florida. Crist had been the attorney general, and one of his campaign promises was to be tough on crime.

One afternoon, a call came from our attorney. He said, "Gene and Carol, Jason's clemency application finally came to the top of the pile, and I've just received word that the Florida Parole Commission has recommended that his case be heard at the next clemency hearing." I was stunned. He continued. "In order to get that hearing, Jason has to be granted a waiver to move forward by the clemency aides. These aides are attorneys and other professionals who work for the four members of the clemency board — the governor, the attorney general, the commissioner of agriculture, and the chief financial officer. The two of you will need to come to Tallahassee to present the case and request the waiver."

My heart was racing. We had been turned down so quickly by the previous administration. Was it possible that God's timing was different from what we expected earlier and that he was still preparing a positive outcome for Jason?

The date came, and we drove the four and a half hours to the state capital. Arriving at the building where the waiver hearing was to take place, we were handed a piece of paper with five cases listed. We were number three. At the top it stated that we would have five minutes to present our case. Anxiety mounted. *Five minutes?* How could it be possible to present the facts of such a huge case in five minutes? We were allowed to be observers as the first two cases were presented. I glanced at my watch. Each of them got fifteen minutes. Perhaps we would too.

It was our turn. My stomach twisted in knots as I took my seat alongside Gene and our attorney. We had a desk in front of us. All eight of the clemency aides were several steps above us, with a large desk in front of them. They could look down on us from a higher vantage point. It was intimidating. Frightening. Nerve-racking.

Our attorney briefly reviewed what the case was about and then said, "Carol, why don't you begin and share what Jason was like in his growing-up years, along with your understanding of what happened, and why you believe he should be given an opportunity for his case to be heard."

I gulped. I felt like I was in the fiery furnace. There was a tremor in my voice as I began to talk about my son. The clemency aides leaned forward, listening intently and asking appropriate questions. Ten minutes into my presentation, I sensed the power of the Holy Spirit in that room. My fear was lessening, and God gave me the courage to respond to the queries from this powerful group of government aides. Then Gene was asked to speak, followed by more questions:

"Are there inmates and family members of inmates who would be willing to write letters in support of your son's work in the prison as an educator, mentor, and positive example?"

"Are there jail and prison volunteers who've gotten to know Jason who would write letters on his behalf?"

"Are there people who have known him before and after his incarceration who would vouch for his character?"

We answered all these questions with an enthusiastic yes.

As the panel began wrapping up our case, they asked us to gather these letters and submit them to the panel so a decision could be made. I looked at my watch. One hour had passed since the panel had begun listening to our case. Our attorney told us that in the history of his work on clemency cases, he had never before seen the panel give that much time to a case at a waiver hearing. Gene and I both sensed the favor of God, and we returned home to begin collecting the requested letters.

It took two months to gather all the letters. One inmate wrote, "I was nothing but a no-good addict before coming to prison, and Jason Kent led me to Jesus Christ." Some of the letters brought me to tears. Clearly, Jason was making a huge difference in the lives of many inmates.

When we finished this task, we put together eight identical notebooks for the clemency aides filled with powerful letters of support. We prayed that God would use the letters to reveal Jason's true character to those who would evaluate whether he would receive a clemency hearing.

Three days later the phone rang. Our attorney said, "I'm sorry to tell you that I've received a form letter from the attorney to the governor, and it's stamped, 'Denied.' Jason will not receive a clemency hearing."

Sobbing, I fell into Gene's arms as he hung up the phone. We had worked and prayed so hard, and we realized there hadn't been time for eight people in the four executive offices to read those notebooks and have a meeting to decide what to do. Jason's case had been given a rubber-stamp denial from the governor's office. It felt like a ridiculous farce that we had even been asked to collect the letters. I was tired of feeling like I'd been kicked in the gut. We knew by law Jason would have to wait another five years to fill out another application for clemency, and it would take another three to five years after that for his paperwork to once again rise to the top of the pile. A hopeless process.

## Delivering the News

The next day was a visitation day. Since we are not allowed to make calls to our son, we would be telling him in person about what had happened. We knew Jason and a committed group of Christian inmate brothers had been fasting and praying on his behalf. I knew this news would be a bitter disappointment for all of them, but especially for Jason.

I was so upset I told Gene I couldn't go with him to the prison in the morning to tell Jason the result. I would come at noon. I was weeping as I finally walked through the second heavy metal door. Jason was waiting for me on the other side. I sobbed into his shoulder. I spoke, choking back the tears, "I'm sorry, son. So much work has been done, and we've prayed so hard. My heart aches for you and your brothers in Christ inside the prison who have fasted and prayed so fervently."

Looking up, I saw the peace of Jesus on Jason's face. Quietly, he said, "Mom, if we were given the waiver and my case was scheduled for a clemency hearing, we might have thought it was because we had the best attorney, or we might have thought it was because we had the favor of politicians." He paused, and with a humble spirit he continued. "The way this has happened, we know the only way I'll ever walk in freedom again in this lifetime is if and when God says I've served enough time and I can help him more outside the razor wire than I can on the inside. And if that never happens on this earth, we need to realize life is short, and we'll all walk in freedom in heaven very soon."

That day my son consoled me, and I came to understand these words from the apostle Paul in a personal and penetrating way:

> And we boast in the hope of the glory of God. Not only so, but we also glory in our sufferings, because we know that suffering produces perseverance; perseverance, character; and character, hope. And hope does not put us to shame, because God's love has been poured out into our hearts through the Holy Spirit, who has been given to us.
>
> ROMANS 5:2 – 5 NIV

Jason understood the power of perseverance — the kind of waiting with hope that is not defined by the immediate results I was praying for.

I was reminded of the three friends who were sentenced to death in a fiery furnace. They said, "If you throw us in the fire, the God we serve can rescue us from your roaring furnace and anything else you might cook up, O king. But *even if he doesn't*, it wouldn't make a bit of difference, O king. *We still wouldn't serve your gods or worship the gold statue you set up*" (Daniel 3:17 – 18, emphasis added). That day I understood that Jason knew God could have rescued him with an eventual end-of-sentence date via the clemency process, but Jason made it clear to me that even if he *never* walked in freedom, he was committed to serving Jesus inside the prison walls.

In the midst of our firestorms, we, too, can reach toward and ask for the enduring faith of Shadrach, Meshach, and Abednego. I am sure they wanted the miracle of *not* being cast into the fire. What horror did they feel as they were thrown into those flames? And what wonder did they feel as God performed an even greater miracle for them, walking with them in the fire and sparing them any damage from the flames and then rescuing them?

Why does God pull off the impossible for some people but not others, even though he is all-powerful? I do not know the answer. But like these three faithful men, and like my son, Jason, I am willing to believe that God is still worthy of my trust. I stand with arms outstretched to heaven and pray, *"Dear Lord, give me the faith to believe you love me, whether I live or die, whether you answer my prayers my way or yours. I choose to believe that you have eternal reasons for every choice you make."*

Could this be a prayer you can pray in your own firestorm? Are you willing to believe that God is still worthy of your trust, no matter how he answers your plea? Would it help if you could catch a glimpse of what awaits you after the firestorm has passed? God already knows the good he has in store for you. Trust him with your hardships and the things you don't understand. Even now, you may be on the brink of new beginnings.

## New Beginnings

No one likes being in the middle of a personal firestorm, but there are often unexpected benefits. *National Geographic* states that even though fires are often harmful and destructive, they also play an integral and beneficial role in nature:

> They return nutrients to the soil by burning dead or decaying matter. They also act as a disinfectant, removing disease-ridden plants and harmful insects from a forest ecosystem. And by burning through thick canopies and brushy undergrowth, fires allow sunlight to reach the forest floor, enabling a new generation of seedlings to grow.

I experienced something like this in my own firestorm. Although it has all the markings of being harmful and destructive, I am also experiencing something new and even surprisingly positive. As the mother of a murderer, I experienced the agony of feeling like a terrible parent. There were days I wanted to hide instead of being open about my journey. My pride was shattered, and I felt like the light had gone out on any hope for the future. But slowly, out of the decaying matter of the past, God birthed new opportunities — for Jason, and for Gene and me.

Jason has now taken over five hundred inmates through Dave Ramsey's Financial Peace University course. He periodically facilitates a biblical counseling class, teaching men how to be good husbands and fathers. And he has a group of inmate brothers in Christ who exercise and pray together. He's the president of "The Gavel Club" and coaches inmates who want to learn how to communicate more effectively.

Jason is sometimes able to connect men who have no caring relatives with families who will write to them, pray for them, and put occasional gifts of money into their inmate accounts for things like personal hygiene items and postage stamps.

When I spoke recently in Cannon Beach, Oregon, a woman I didn't initially recognize reminded me we had met four years earlier at the same conference center. She and her husband had asked if Jason knew an inmate who needed encouragement, and while there, I was able to get the name and address of an inmate Jason recommended. She handed me this note:

> *Dear Carol,*
>
> *Thank you for giving me the name of Gary through your son. My husband and I have faithfully written to him for the past four years, and God has knitted our hearts together. Just recently Gary asked if I would be his earthly mother.*
>
> *Gary met Jesus Christ in prison. Then he finished his high school education, and now we are sponsoring him as he successfully journeys through Bible school while he is incarcerated.*
>
> *Gary is now my son through Christ, and his weekly letters bless me in a way only Jesus can ordain. Your Jason has sent me notes of encouragement, too, and I pray for him and their prayer group, as well as for you and your husband.*
>
> *Because of Him,*
> *Cat*

This unexpected connection with Cat was a reminder to me of the powerful way God is bringing new life out of our firestorm. Gene and I have chosen to go public with our story, and we hear from people all over the world who are struggling with a wide variety of devastating personal challenges. At a conference in Florida, a woman said, "Carol, my son is incarcerated, and I was so ashamed that I hid from people in my neighborhood and in my church. When I read your story in *When I Lay My Isaac Down*, I realized you put what I've been feeling into words. For the first time, I didn't feel alone, and I'm going to start being transparent about what I'm going through. I know God wants to birth new hope from my experience too."

Daily, I'm discovering that one of God's specialties is allowing his light to reach the barren, deadened places of my impossible situation. And out of what looks like devastation come new growth, fresh faith, richer relationships, and unexpected opportunities to ignite renewed hope in the lives of others. It's an adventure like nothing I've experienced before. The worst fire does indeed prepare the way for a new beginning.

## COME TO THE FIRE

1. What is the worst firestorm you've ever faced in your life? How long did it last? Did you feel comfortable talking to someone about it, or did you feel alone?
2. Shadrach, Meshach, and Abednego experienced a miraculous intervention, and they came out of the fiery furnace unscathed. In the middle of a life-threatening situation, these men said that even if God didn't rescue them, they would remain faithful

to him. What would it look like for you to have faith in the midst of a gigantic obstacle? What frightens you and intrigues you about that possibility?

3. Carol's family experienced a discouraging time when God did not answer their prayers for an eventual end-of-sentence date for their son. Has there been a time in your life when it appeared God didn't answer your prayers or answered them in a totally different way than you expected? How did that experience impact your faith?

4. Firestorms in nature have unexpected benefits because nutrients are returned to the soil and disease-ridden plants are destroyed. In your life, what unexpected benefits or new beginnings has God brought about after a difficult experience?

## FIRE-BUILDING CHALLENGE

This week, contact someone you know who has been through a challenging experience and has come through with vibrant faith. Ask if they've gone through a time when their faith wavered, and what happened to rekindle their trust in God. What faith-building lessons did they learn, and what unanticipated benefits or blessings did they experience?

# CHAPTER 3

# Enduring Embers

When God calls ... he bids [us] come and burn—burn
with a new love, a new desire, that will take all the mixed
and muddled desires and ambitions and burn till it has
refined all that was God-given in them and purged out all
that was going in the other direction.

**N. T. Wright,** *The Crown and the Fire*

The envelope looked official, and it was addressed to me. The
return address indicated it was from the Clerk of the Court.
Uneasy, I slid the document from the envelope and unfolded
it. The first word that blared at me from the top of the legal-
size letter was SUMMONS. The large type and bold lettering
looked like a threat—like a word screaming at me from a piece
of paper. There was no "Dear Carol" or any other kind of salu-
tation before the first paragraph:

> *By order of the Circuit and County Courts of Polk County,
> Florida, you are hereby summoned to appear for jury ser-
> vice. Any person who is summoned to attend as a juror in
> any court and who fails to attend without any sufficient*

*excuse shall pay a fine ... Report to the Jury Assembly Room, 2nd Floor, Polk County Courthouse, 255 North Broadway Avenue, Bartow, FL, on 2/20/12 at 8:05 a.m.*

My heart started palpitating, my hands were ice-cold, and I had trouble breathing. I hadn't been inside a courtroom in almost ten years — not since my son was convicted of first-degree murder in 2002, with journalists pointing microphones in my direction and Court TV cameras in my face, trying to get an emotional sound bite from the tear-stained face of a criminal's mother. I felt like throwing up. Weakness swept over my body, and I felt too sick to function normally. Placing the letter on the island in my kitchen, I walked outside to get some air.

My thoughts swirled. "Surely the government does not require that a mother who has gone through everything I've experienced in a courtroom would have to go back, become part of a jury, and try to make a decision about the guilt or innocence of someone else's loved one. That would be cruel and unusual punishment. I cannot watch a woman sitting where I sat in a courtroom — agonizing over the future of her son, daughter, or husband." I got a lump in my throat just imagining what it would be like — the sadness, the irony, the vicarious grief, and the heart-twisting decision making.

Walking back inside, I picked up the summons, looking for the place on the form where I could decline participation. Scanning the page, I found a section titled "Request for Excusal/Postponement." I suddenly felt better, knowing there was a provision for being excused. But then I read further. The only reasons for not showing up for jury selection didn't fit me.

I'm not an illegal alien; I'm not under prosecution for a crime; I don't work in law enforcement; I'm not the sole provider for a child under six years old; I'm not seventy or older; I'm not in the military, nor am I a practicing attorney or physician. I'm not suffering from a medical impairment, nor am I responsible for someone incapable of caring for himself or herself.

There was one final option — a box to check if I wanted to have my jury duty postponed *one* time, to be rescheduled for a future week within the next two to six months. I checked *that* box and wrote the date of April 2, 2012, as the Monday I would report for duty. The date I picked was just a few days before Easter, and I figured the courts would be shut down most of that week so judges and attorneys could have a spring break.

I was wrong.

On the morning I needed to appear in the courthouse, I scanned my closet for appropriate clothing. Once again memories engulfed me as I thought about the day I was getting ready to testify about my son's mental state before he committed the murder. I remembered thinking, "I shouldn't look too business-like or I might look threatening to someone on the jury. My earrings should be simple, not sparkly or dangling. Should I wear a skirt or slacks? Should I wear heels or flats? Should I wear my usual makeup? I should definitely not wear the belt with the big shiny buckle. Could my appearance hurt my son in any way?"

Amid the mental gymnastics of remembering the last courthouse I was in, I threw on a pair of black slacks and a classic blazer, along with low-heeled, simple black boots and small gold earrings. I applied a little makeup, prayed with Gene, and drove the thirty miles to the courthouse.

Once inside, my anxiety mounted. I was given a "panel

number," the name of a judge for which my group of prospective jurors would be considered, and a form to fill out. We watched a short movie about our civic duty and the privilege of serving on a jury. Given my history, I didn't feel it was a privilege at all. It was an obligation I wanted to escape. One by one, juror panels were sent to courtrooms to be evaluated for potential service. At eleven o'clock, my group was called, and we were taken up an elevator to the top floor of the courthouse. Our guide said, "This is the floor where the really bad cases get tried."

Panic seized my heart. *"God, help me! I can't do this,"* I silently prayed.

The guide continued, "However, this week we have so many lesser crimes to handle that we've moved some of them up to this floor."

I sighed with relief. "At least I won't have to decide if someone should get the death penalty or a sentence of life without the possibility of parole," I thought.

The judge greeted us with courtesy and respect and thanked us for our service. Then the defendant, his attorney, and the prosecutor filed in, and shortly thereafter both attorneys began questioning members of the jury pool. People were attentive and polite as they responded to the queries the attorneys had after reading through our questionnaires.

Suddenly, one of the attorneys looked up and said, "Mrs. Kent?" I jolted to attention and raised my hand as I nodded in his direction. He continued. "I see you and your family have had an experience in the courtroom. Do you think that would in any way influence your ability to evaluate a case fairly if you were a member of a jury?"

I felt a flush come to my face, and my breathing was labored.

"Well," I stammered, "my son is a graduate of the U.S. Naval Academy, and he married a previously married woman with two children …" Instead of saying a simple yes or no, for the next three minutes I went on and on and on, providing way too much information. It was as if a floodgate had opened, and I poured out information, trying to bring some dignity to my incarcerated son. I ended with, "Jason was convicted of murder and sentenced to life in prison — so I can honestly say my experience with the court system would definitely influence how I process information during a trial."

A hush fell over the room as my fellow jury pool members looked at me with new eyes, seeing me as the mother of a convicted murderer. I was asked follow-up questions about whether or not I could remove myself from personal feelings from my past experience and be a fair juror. I told the attorney I could be fair. Then we were dismissed for a break.

Standing in the hallway, I found myself alone. Groups of three or four other people huddled together in different parts of the waiting area, talking softly and glancing in my direction. I had no doubt they were talking about me. I could only imagine what they were saying about my shocking response to a simple question. It was the first time since the week of Jason's trial that I felt totally excluded. Judged. Alienated. Gossiped about. Humiliated. I was an outcast. It felt unfair and hurtful. I can't think of a time when I was more in need of a kind word from someone — *anyone*!

Within a short time we were told that the case we were assigned to had been resolved with a plea bargain, and we were dismissed. As we left the courthouse, no one walked with me to the parking lot or made me feel like a part of the shared experience of showing up for jury duty. On the drive home, I felt a new wall go up between God and me. I, of course, was the one who pulled away.

Over the next few weeks I struggled. My spiritual fervor was not raging with its usual intensity, and I didn't feel any excitement about my dreams of what I could do to further God's kingdom on earth. I still believed in God and embraced Jesus as my Savior — that hadn't changed. I was still confident in God's trustworthy character and his love for me. But my spiritual passion seemed more of a smolder than a bright burn.

## The Ebb and Flow of Faith

Over the years, I have come to realize that my Christian life has an ebb and flow to it. There are times I experience great joy in my relationship with God — when I sense his smile of approval on my life and ministry, and I'm encouraged by the doors he is opening and the loving relationships I've been given. But there are other times, like my experience of humiliation in the courthouse, when I sense the fire of my faith slipping into a slow burn. I know God is with me; I'm not in crisis; and my fire hasn't gone out — but the intensity of my faith and my emotional connection with God seem to dwindle from high to low.

Is that wrong? Is it failure when the challenges of life seem to douse our feelings of closeness with God and deaden our senses for the One who created us, saved us, and offers the power to sustain us?

My friend Cindy, who has walked with the Lord through many heartrending trials over the years, has gained a perspective on this question that sustains her through dark times.

Prior to the age of forty, my faith survived firestorms like infertility, the loss of babies, several surgeries and serious health challenges, the demands of a high-risk adoption, that son's addictions and disappearances, and the departure of that son in his mid-teens as he chose to leave us as his parents and go back to a poverty-stricken, addicted mother. I really thought I'd seen the worst that life could throw at me, and, since God strengthened my faith and endurance through all of those trials, I was certain the "victorious Christian life" was mine to enjoy forever. My faith had grown deep and wide and steady.

But at age forty and thereafter, I experienced one shattering experience after another — my husband's abandonment, an unwanted divorce, severe depression and anxiety, a major career shift, the pressures of corporate politics run amok, overwhelming job demands, more surgeries and health crises, my son's imprisonment, taking on the parenting of a grandchild, watching a stepdaughter go into harm's way in war zones for multiple one-year deployments, and my new husband's severe health crises.

In these difficulties, I found myself up against a far different type of challenge — my own personal limitations of strength, performance, skills, endurance, and energy in spite of my faith. God's answers to my prayers were not to fix the situations or fill me with supernatural abilities to meet the challenges and save the day. Instead, as I plowed forward through these trials, I saw my personal failures like I'd never seen them before — and found myself disappointed in myself. How different it was to battle personal failures rather than external challenges. Both hurt; both can be crushing; both can be marvelous crucibles for God to burn out the dross and purify us; both can help us see God more clearly and our need for a Savior more acutely. But the pain of disappointment in myself added a weight that dragged me down lower.

In truth, the challenges since the age of forty humbled me far more than the ones prior to forty. I have felt my cheeks burn with humiliation, been disappointed in myself, seen myself fall short of my own goals and the goals of others when the onslaught of demands and challenges proved larger than my capacity to meet them, even with my faith and prayer life rich and deep and solid. Even with the best of intentions and bringing all my experience and heart and soul to bear. Maybe that is just part of the maturation process; maybe it's that our humility grows with age. We learn to live with our limitations. I do know, though, that I am richer for it.

I know exactly what Cindy means. The storms I faced and endured before Jason's crime left me feeling roused to heights of courage and victory. I'd faced the lions in the den, then come out stronger for it. But the ongoing challenges of Jason's imprisonment not only shook me to my core; they lingered day after day, month after month, year after year, and repeatedly exposed my greatest weaknesses. They humbled me and required me to not fight a single blazing battle to win a victory, but instead to navigate my way through a long endurance test. I knew Cindy's faith was solid, so how did this experience affect her spiritual passion? She continued:

As I worshiped the God of the resurrection this Easter, I would have liked to have felt waves of emotional passion, deep stirrings of goose-bump awe, and exuberant celebration over my risen Lord. I didn't. And in light of the discussions you and I have been having about wildfire faith, Carol, I asked myself if that meant my flame was flickering too low.

But I decided that is not what it meant at all.

My worship that morning wasn't the leaping flames of a newly lit fire, spreading over green wood still moist and unscarred by flame. My worship was a solid bed of burning hot coals that have long simmered in the heart of the fire. You know, you can throw a branch on the top of a bonfire and watch new flame lick its bark and ignite into bright, dancing tongues of yellow, blue, and white, but if you catch it early enough, you can grab that branch back out of the fire with your bare hands, toss it on the dirt, step on it, and put the flame out in just a moment, and *maybe* your hand will get just a little burned in the process.

But you can't reach into a fire and grab one of those dark red glowing embers in the bed of that fire. They are too hot to handle. Anything that touches them instantly ignites. One touch and you are scorched with severe burns. Those embers are way past the bright bursts of leaping yellow and blue flames. The fire lives in their core. They've been consumed by the fire to the point they *are* the heart that keeps that fire burning, even when the bright, leaping flames are doused by rain or snuffed out by wind or shrink down for lack of new wood.

This fifty-something woman who knows what it is to disappoint herself and others, who looks in the mirror and knows her frailties and limitations but also knows that God loves, enjoys, delights in, and even celebrates her fellowship—this woman understands her need for a Savior of grace far better than the twenty-year-old she once was, when her faith was fresher but untested, when her exuberance ran high as she grew by leaps and bounds but hadn't yet felt the crush of pain this life can heap on us.

It's like the difference between the romance of a new love that makes a couple flush with excitement just at the sight of each other and the romance of a mature love that leads a couple to reach for one another's hands and squeeze in partnership while walking into a jail to see their son, or into the hospital room to say good-bye to a dying parent, or into a military complex to hug a daughter good-bye on her way to war, or into the medical center for a test or procedure, or even, on the bright side, into the nursery to play with a newborn grandchild. Young love knows bursts of excitement and thrill; mature love knows deep satisfaction, bedrock joy, and undying loyalty.

Embers are the mature heart of the fire that keeps it going. They will do their work of igniting new wood when new fuel is thrown on the fire, but in between those times they will bury themselves under the gray ashes and allow the fire to slowly burn itself deeper and deeper into their core.

I believe Cindy is on to something here. I asked above, "Is it failure when the challenges of life seem to douse our feelings of closeness with God and deaden our senses for the One who created us, saved us, and offers the power to sustain us?" No, I don't believe that is failure at all. We must never confuse *feelings* with *faith*. When our feelings wane — and they will, for all sorts of reasons — we must stir through the ashes to reveal the glowing embers of our still-living faith. Embers, I have discovered, are critically important to an enduring wildfire faith.

## Enduring Embers
## Are the Keepers of the Flame

So what are embers? I used to think of embers as the sad remains of a dying fire. And from one perspective, that is true. Left alone, embers *will* eventually burn themselves out. But discovering more about the science of embers has changed my perspective entirely.

According to Reference.com, embers are the glowing, hot coals made of greatly heated wood, coal, or other carbon-based material that precede or remain after a fire. Embers can burn very hot, sometimes just as hot as the fire itself. They continue to radiate a substantial amount of heat long after the fire has gone out. In cooking, embers are often preferred over open flame because they radiate a more constant form of heat than an open fire.

An ember is usually formed when a fire has only partially consumed a piece of fuel and some usable chemical energy still remains. Often that usable chemical energy is left because it is so deep into the center of the material that air does not reach it, which means it hasn't yet fully combusted. The reason embers continue to stay hot is that combustion is still happening on a miniature scale. The small yellow, orange, and red glowing lights often seen within embers are actually combustion. That's why embers are so dangerous in forest fires. With the right wind conditions, embers can be blown far ahead of the fire front, igniting spot fires hundreds of yards away.

Now consider these facts in connection with the embers of our faith. Embers are created in one place only — the intense heat of trials — where all of our external resources have been burned away. The fire that has infiltrated our core is kept alive deep inside where the air cannot reach it. Here, the fire of our faith can burn evenly and slowly, radiating constant trust. Embers keep the power of the fire safe, awaiting one of three things — time to finally flicker out, new fuel to ignite the fire afresh, or a wind to lift the embers and carry them to fresh fuel, even great distances away, where our faith springs to life anew.

Keep all of this information in mind as we take a look at the words of Jesus in Matthew 5, traditionally referred to as the Beatitudes. I often turn to this passage when my life feels disappointing or when I feel judged by people who find out my son is in prison for murder.

When Jesus saw his ministry drawing huge crowds, he climbed a hillside. Those who were apprenticed to him, the committed, climbed with him. [I love that image. I want to "climb with him" too!] Arriving at a quiet place, he sat down and taught his climbing companions. This is what he said:

"You're blessed when you're at the end of your rope. With less of you there is more of God and his rule.

"You're blessed when you feel you've lost what is most dear to you. Only then can you be embraced by the One most dear to you.

"You're blessed when you're content with just who you are—no more, no less. That's the moment you find yourselves proud owners of everything that can't be bought.

"You're blessed when you've worked up a good appetite for God. He's food and drink in the best meal you'll ever eat.

"You're blessed when you care. At the moment of being 'care-full,' you find yourselves cared for.

"You're blessed when you get your inside world—your mind and heart—put right. Then you can see God in the outside world.

"You're blessed when you can show people how to cooperate instead of compete or fight. That's when you discover who you really are, and your place in God's family.

"You're blessed when your commitment to God provokes persecution. The persecution drives you even deeper into God's kingdom.

"Not only that — count yourselves blessed every time people put you down or throw you out or speak lies about you to discredit me. What it means is that the truth is too close for comfort and they are uncomfortable. You can be glad when that happens — give a cheer, even! — for though they don't like it, *I* do! And all heaven applauds. And know that you are in good company. My prophets and witnesses have always gotten into this kind of trouble."

MATTHEW 5:1 – 12

Every principle Jesus teaches here begins with "You're blessed when ..." The word *blessed* means "to be favored with supreme happiness." In other words, when we suffer, yet take the teaching of Jesus into the core of our being, we are right on target for total joy in this life and in the next.

As I read Jesus' words, I see the connections he makes between hardships — the firestorms of life — and the enduring embers of a faith that can go on burning to produce great results. Take a moment to review the passage again, focusing on the trials — the setbacks, sufferings, broken dreams — that Jesus tells us bring about such deep rewards and can actually make us stronger and even happier. Jesus knew it is only when the fire burns away the easily combustible material — those weak parts of us — that the fire has a chance to infiltrate our core, making us hot coals that will endure over time rather than useless ash that will simply blow away.

This means when bad things happen — or when I'm hurt, offended, misunderstood, or even simply discontent — I can know there are spiritual rewards that will serve me well and enable me to impact the world in ways I never otherwise could have.

## Embers We Can Depend On

One of my dearest friends, Carrie, experienced the bittersweet reality of one of those powerful principles: "You're blessed when you feel you've lost what is most dear to you. Only then can you be embraced by the One most dear to you" (Matthew 5:4). She shared these words:

My husband of twenty-eight years sat silently beside me, unmoved by my tears. He was on one of his visits to our home since announcing he wanted out of the marriage. Each time he came, I hoped we could end this awful nightmare and rekindle our relationship. Instead, he managed to find new ways to rip the scab off a heart that was trying to heal. Surely, if I just let him know!

I took a deep breath and continued. "Honey, I'm dying inside. All that's holding our marriage together is my love for you. Please, just a look, a touch, a word—don't let it die!"

His blank look morphed into a haughty grin.

"I know exactly what you want and need," he said. "I could make you the happiest woman in the world, just like that!" He snapped his fingers. "But," he added flatly, "I don't want to." He got up and walked away.

My dreams had turned to ashes. I wondered how I would survive as I hopelessly surveyed the charred remains of the life I once knew. We were more than best friends; we were kindred spirits. We dated through his pilot training and kept love letters flying between Vietnam and grad school. We were thrilled when at last he landed on U.S. soil, and we were married. The military immediately whisked us overseas for our first four-year assignment. Our adventures of traveling and starting a family, as well as tragic losses of babies and loved ones, all seemed to bring us closer together as a couple. Five years into marriage, we became Christians, and a whole new dimension of life began. He became an elder, teaching and preaching, leading people to Christ. I became involved in women's ministries, all while we were raising our children together in a Christ-centered home. Life was good. Our twenty-three years in the Air Force flew by. We eventually returned to the U.S. and to his exciting new career as a commercial pilot. But soon, his trips became longer and more frequent, keeping him away from home more and more.

"Been called out on a trip!" he'd say, and off he'd go, putting his sports car into gear and zooming away, usually for days at a time. I never had any cause to question or distrust. I just figured it was all part of the job and was happy he was doing what he loved.

Until one Sunday afternoon. I remember exactly where we were standing in the kitchen when I heard my husband's words:

"I don't love you. I never loved you. I have something else going on ... You're not part of it ... I'm leaving."

I was stunned. Hadn't we just held hands in church that morning? Hadn't we been leading marriage seminars together? I was met by steely eyes and an emotional gut punch that sent me reeling. I stumbled up the stairs, doubled over as a wave of nausea swept over me. I passed by my daughter's room where she lay peacefully napping.

I can't do this. I can't tell her. *God, please help me! No! Don't let this be true! Help us!*

Can you imagine Carrie's pain? Where does a woman go when, in an instant, her world has gone up in flames, and the man she loves — the husband, the daddy — is the one who lit the match? Carrie continued:

Agony of the soul. Heartache. Simple phrases that defy description. I'd never known there could be a literal ache in my heart, an indescribable crushing pain inside that strikes at the deepest level.

Gradually, my husband's double life had become our pattern of life. The trust, security, and laughter we once shared had given way to addiction and adultery. Our Christ-centered home had become a place where lies and deceit wormed their way into the heart of our marriage.

"Leave him. You have biblical grounds," urged a counselor and people who knew my husband well.

"I know God may lead others to do so," I'd respond, "but he hasn't yet given me peace about it."

This was true. I did not want to divorce. I know what it does to families. As a child of a broken home, I couldn't bear the thought of my children going through that pain. I desperately wanted to keep our family intact, and hoped we could restore what we once had together. And so I watched and waited for the knight in shining armor to gallop in on his white steed and rescue our marriage. He never came.

Incredibly, it was nearly nine years before my husband officially left — nine years before divorce papers and a judge's gavel declared our marriage dead. That very next day, curled up on the bed between two fluffy pillows, I numbly reached for my pen and journal and slowly began pouring out my heart to God through muffled cries for his help. Even in my pain, I knew from years in God's Word that I was covered by his amazing grace. Praising, singing, shedding tears off and on—in worship I found the reminder of the goodness of God. I was covered by God's amazing grace. He was my Husband now.

Over time, in my weakness I found his strength. My circumstances would not change, but I would. My God was doing something special, and I didn't want to miss it. In his Word, I found life and peace, comfort and direction.

Carrie's description of the truths she held on to is a perfect example of the enduring embers of her faith that could not be extinguished by the heartbreaking crisis she was facing. And she fed more heat to those embers with the fuel of God's Word. Watch now for one very special ember that emerges from her excruciating fire:

So what happened in those nine years—those 3,141 days between the "bomb" and the "burial" of our marriage? What did God do with me during those 75,384 hours in his waiting-room-turned-classroom? You need only to peek into my well-worn Bible and my journals—dozens of them—for the answer. Some have crinkled pages, shaky lettering, and other telltale signs of tearful entries. They are filled to the brim with timely, life-giving Scriptures. James knew what he was talking about when he wrote, "Draw near to God and He will draw near to you" (James 4:8 NASB).

Though I would never have willingly signed up for this trial, I would never trade any of the lessons I have learned. One of the most difficult, yet most necessary, lessons God taught me was this: Forgiveness does not change the past, but it expands our future. It's not instant; it's not easy—this process of forgiveness. I doubt it's even fully possible apart from the redemptive work of God within us.

Two years after the divorce, I stood face-to-face with my former husband and his second wife at a family event.

"I'm sorry for all the pain and disappointment I caused you," he said softly, words I thought I would never hear. "I hope you can forgive me someday."

"I already have—long ago," I smiled. "But thank you for that."

"One thing about you—you always were a good forgiver," he replied.

If that's true, it is a powerful tribute to the God who worked in my heart, over time, to bring it about. God was true to his promise in Isaiah: "If it seems like you're walking through fire with flames licking at your limbs, keep going; you won't be burned. Because I, the Eternal One, am your God ... Watch closely: I am preparing something new ... a way through the desert" (Isaiah 43:2–3, 19 The Voice).

Do you see the embers she found, like treasures, buried in the ashes? I can see two—her love of God's Word and her experience of forgiveness. What embers are still glowing in your ash heap?

## The Power of Embers

I believe Cindy's and Carrie's experiences illustrate a critically important principle for developing an unquenchable faith. For faith to endure over time, it needs to develop embers, and those embers are created only by intense heat that is so relentless that the remaining signs of life are deeply buried within the soul. The fire keeps reaching deeper, which in turn keeps the heat alive, just waiting for new fuel it can ignite.

There is an inescapable paradox here. The hardships Jesus

names in Matthew 5 are often considered the end of happiness, yet they are actually the beginning of a richer joy. In the same way, embers are often associated with the dying out of a fire, what we might think of as "the remains" of a fire. But in reality, they are the lingering *life* of the fire, not its death. Embers are the last to hold on to the blaze, and they wait, ready for new fuel to ignite a fresh blaze of bright fire.

Through challenging circumstances, Cindy, Carrie, and I kept feeding new fuel to the embers of our faith over a period of years. The fuel was prayer, the Word of God, fellowship with his people, and intentionally reaching toward God rather than running from him when pain, disappointment, heartache, and brokenness threatened to consume us. And now that fuel — ignited by those stubborn, lingering embers — has produced new flames of life and new embers, allowing the hot bed of the fire to keep burning on and on and on.

This understanding of the nature and purpose of the embers of our faith can inspire us to feed our faith in a few specific ways.

1. *Welcome your trials as gifts.* Hardships build strength and endurance that will help you to burn long and hot, able to withstand spells when no new fuel comes for a long time. So when you encounter those trials, call on God, crying out to him, always moving toward him and not away from him. Know he will use every experience for your eternal good.

2. *Allow the heat of your embers to warm your spirit.* You can do this, as Carrie did, by holding on to everything you know to be true of God's character. She turned to God's Word; she practiced forgiveness; she

drew near to God in prayer. Internalize the truth that even if you don't see bright new flames blazing, his "slow burn" is digging into your core, generating light and heat that will endure over time. When trouble comes (and it will), meditate on who God is and his eternal love for you. In so doing, you will allow the embers of your soul to retain their heat, even when you feel you have no energy left to keep going.

3. *Never stop seeking out new fuel.* Don't starve your embers. Feed them! Feed them through worship and fellowship, through acts of kindness that spread the fire to others, just as Jason now teaches Bible studies and classes for other inmates. Before long, as our embers spark new fires in the lives of others, we begin to blaze again, amazed at how God's wildfire faith spreads from life to life.

Now, armed with your new understanding of the enduring power of embers and the important role they play in keeping our faith alive and spreading it to others, you are more equipped than ever to grow your faith into a wildfire faith that endures anything. In the next chapter, we'll discover that enduring hardship isn't the only pathway to spiritual growth.

## COME TO THE FIRE

1. Even though she had a personal relationship with God for many years, Carol experienced a diminished trust in him and questioned why he allowed her to go through the difficult experience of being called for jury duty. Sometimes our faith-fire seems red-hot and

at other times it seems dim. But there are enduring embers — the mature heart of the fire — ready to be stoked. In what way do you identify with this "ebb and flow" of faith?

2. Read through Jesus' words from Matthew 5 again (pages 72–73). Which of the "You're blessed when" statements do you identify with most right now? Why? In what ways, if any, are you experiencing God's blessing in the middle of your challenging circumstances? If you don't recognize God's favor yet, how do you hope he might bless you in this situation?

3. Cindy makes a distinction between young and old love as she describes the significance of embers. How do you relate this analogy to your own relationship with God? What does it take to hold on to mature faith when nothing about life seems easy or fair?

4. Carrie itemized the valuable lessons she learned in the fire and referred to her long period of devastation as a classroom where she learned to forgive a husband who betrayed her. If you think of your difficult circumstances as a classroom, how would you describe the "lessons" you are learning?

## FIRE-BUILDING CHALLENGE

Identify a time when your faith seemed to be in a slow burn rather than bright and vibrant. Based on that experience, make a list of benefits that can come from a time when your faith is in the embers stage.

# CHAPTER 4

# Burning Bushes

Do you remember Moses at the burning bush?
God had to tell him to take off his shoes—he didn't
know he was on holy ground. And if we can just come
to see that right where we are is holy ground—in our jobs
and homes, with our coworkers and friends and families.
This is where we learn to pray.

Richard J. Foster, *Prayer*

The call was unexpected. The voice on the other end of the line was the superintendent of schools in the district where I had taught junior high drama, speech, and English for four years prior to the birth of my son. I had taken the last year off to be a stay-at-home mom. "Why is he calling me?" I wondered.

He was direct. "Carol, we have an opening for a teacher to direct the alternative education program at the Project 23 house, and I'm wondering if you would be interested in that position. I feel what's been lacking in that program to date is any kind of a spiritual emphasis, and I believe you could bring that element to the girls who are in the program."

The Newaygo County Intermediate School District in Michigan had developed an education program for unwed pregnant teens a few years earlier. The plan was for these girls to enter a different kind of learning experience during their pregnancies and for the semester following the birth of their babies. As the director of the program, my job would be to tailor the curriculum so these girls could stay in school during a time when many in similar circumstances tended to drop out. The year was 1975, a time when societal pressures on unwed teens were much more intense than they are today.

The program was affectionately referred to as Project 23 because of the address of the house provided for the program, marked by two aging number plaques — a 2 and a 3 — dangling precariously beside the front door. It was adjacent to other school property and had been purchased for future expansion, but for the time being, it offered a home setting while the girls continued their education and learned how to care for their babies at the same time. They lived in their own homes and were bused to the Project 23 house five days a week. The students were either pregnant or new mothers, and those with newborns often brought their babies to school with them.

The call from the superintendent hit me like a bolt of lightning. It was a burning bush moment — unexpected, supernatural, God-powered. God was opening a door where there had been no door, giving me the opportunity to invest my expertise and passion in an area of teaching that made my heart sing. Because babies were welcomed at the Project 23 house, it also meant that during the off-school hours when I would be spending extra time tutoring the girls, my own baby son could often be with me.

Within a week I had accepted the position, and everything was official. I was named the director of the Alternative Education Program for Pregnant Teenagers. The following September,

I was ready to take on my new mission. School was starting right after Labor Day, and I readied the Project 23 house for its occupants. With its large table, the dining room was our main classroom. The kitchen was the perfect spot for classes in nutrition. The living room was well suited for small group activities and counseling, and the remaining room became my office.

On the first day of school, I arrived early and stood in the living room and prayed, *"Lord, thank you for this incredible job. As each of my students enters this home, help her to feel your presence and to know that no matter what she's been through or how worthless she feels, you love her and have a plan for her life and her baby's life far beyond what she can see right now. Help her to value the life of that baby and to know that in spite of her current circumstances, you can give her a reason to go on."*

I walked through every room in the house, praying as I walked. *"Lord, help me to love the least likable girl who walks through this door in the same way I care for the most charming and personable young woman. Help them to see your reflection in me as I teach."*

At that moment, I had no idea that over the next two years, sixty-eight teenage girls would come and go through the Project 23 door. During my last year of directing the program, seven of my students were only fourteen years old when they gave birth to their first child.

At times my mission seemed wondrous. I was able to speak freely about the value of life and bring in professionals representing adoption agencies. Nutrition experts donated their services to train the girls. A myriad of doctors and nurses gave their time to affect young lives at Project 23. And I was passionate about sharing my faith. I knew this teaching opportunity was a marker moment in my life — an opportunity to walk in the direction of God's leading in his power and might in a way that would produce lasting change in the lives of my students.

But slowly, I realized that listening was more important than teaching. The more comfortable the girls were with me, the more honest they became. Their comments pierced my heart. "I have never heard my parents say the words 'I love you' to me. I planned this pregnancy so I could finally have somebody love me back." "This is my second baby. I killed my first one with an abortion. I felt such guilt I decided to have this one to make up for the one I murdered."

And so there were discouraging days too.

Two of my teen moms had babies two years in a row. Was I doing anything that made a difference in their lives? Was I wasting my time? Obviously, my influence had done nothing to change the way they made decisions. I needed to reconnect with God and receive a fresh vision of my purpose and mission. Slowly, when I stopped long enough to listen, God nudged my heart with a new thought.

He was telling me to keep planting seeds of kindness and love in the lives of my girls without always attaching a sermon or expecting instant results. He didn't appear in a burning bush, but he spoke to my heart clearly: *"Carol, I opened this opportunity for you. Represent me in this place by teaching well and by loving these girls. They will see my reflection through you. Remember my faithfulness to you in the past. Leave the results with me."* The weekend when I realized what he was saying, I sat at my desk and opened my Bible to a passage I hadn't referred to in a long time. The words pierced my heart. In a more recent paraphrase, it reads:

I'll never forget the trouble, the utter lostness,
    the taste of ashes ...
I remember it all ...
    the feeling of hitting the bottom.
But there's one other thing I remember,
    and remembering, I keep a grip on hope:
GOD's loyal love couldn't have run out,
    his merciful love couldn't have dried up.
They're created new every morning.
    How great your faithfulness!
I'm sticking with GOD ...
    He's all I've got left.
GOD proves to be good to the man who passionately
    waits,
    to the woman who diligently seeks.
It's a good thing to quietly hope,
    quietly hope for help from GOD.

                              LAMENTATIONS 3:19 – 26

I felt reassured by God's Word that I needed to wait patiently on God — that he, not I, would bring change into the lives of these girls.

The next Monday morning, I arrived at the house to find two of my students there early. They sat around the kitchen table discussing how hard motherhood was.

One said, "I thought little babies just ate and slept, and all my baby does is cry."

The other responded, "I know what you mean. The father of my baby has already taken off, and this mother stuff is hard."

Spontaneously, I spoke up and said, "Girls, I just learned the neatest little song. It sounds like you could use a lift today. Do you mind if I sing it to you?"

Jackie, the more sarcastic of the two, looked up with a sneer and said, "You want to sing us a song — *on Monday morning?* You have got to be kidding!"

Jeannie shrugged as she rolled her eyes at me and then back at Jackie as she patronizingly said, "Oh, come on; let's let her sing."

I looked at them, smiled, and started to sing simple lyrics with a made-up tune: "God loves you and I love you and that's the way it should be. God loves you and I love you and that's the way it is." I gave each of them a hug, but said nothing more.

Moments later, with tears in her eyes, Jeannie looked up and said, "I haven't been to church in a long time. Do you think you could pick me up so I could go to church with you next Sunday?"

Jackie was still stoic, and without eye contact she spoke. "I haven't been to church in a long time either. Do you think you could pick me up too?"

The next Sunday I drove both girls, along with their babies, to church. I was filled with hope that this service might be a turning point for one or both of them. We talked and laughed on the way. After dropping off their babies in the nursery, we found seats in the sanctuary.

The service was excellent — great worship, powerful preaching, and a sense of God's Spirit moving in hearts. The gospel message was clear, and the sermon was easy to follow. I waited expectantly, and nothing happened. *Nothing.*

I don't know if Jackie or Jeannie ever received Christ; they never asked to go to church with me again. But I know they heard his message of love and forgiveness that day. I learned that my role in God's kingdom is to see every day as an opportunity to embrace the holy ground I'm standing on, to fully understand that no act of kindness or demonstration of love is ever wasted, whether or not I see tangible results.

Sometimes I confuse wildfire faith with emotional feelings or visible outcomes. But experiencing passionate faith doesn't mean shivers, happiness, excitement, bubbling emotion, or reporting on how many people "prayed the prayer." It doesn't mean we always see profound results when we have labored long and prayed hard. True wildfire faith means having strength, endurance, and a solid abiding trust in God — in darkness and in light, in pain and in wellness, in sadness and in laughter. It is recognizing that today, no matter where I am or what my circumstances may be, because I am the image bearer of Jesus Christ, the ground I'm standing on is holy ground.

Of all the people who have ever lived, perhaps Moses had the most experience with standing on holy ground.

## From the Burning Bush to the Wilderness

Moses was saved from sure death by a God-fearing, creative mama who hid him for three months before coating a papyrus basket with tar and pitch, placing him in the basket, and hiding it along the reeds in the Nile River. We love the story of Pharaoh's daughter going to the river to bathe and then discovering an adorable baby who was irresistible. That day God did the impossible — he saved Baby Moses from death, arranged for his biological mother to be his nurse, and prompted a princess to raise him as her son. It sounds like fodder for a fairy tale.

But Moses' life was far from fantasy. At this time in biblical history, the Israelites were slaves doing hard labor. Moses grew up as a prince in the palace, but then in the heat of anger at seeing an Egyptian beating a Hebrew slave, he murdered the

Egyptian and fled to Midian. Moses married and had a child. Many years later, the king of Egypt died. As I read this story in Exodus, I felt the pain it expresses:

> The Israelites groaned under their slavery and cried out. Their cries for relief from their hard labor ascended to God:
> God listened to their groanings.
> God remembered his covenant with Abraham, with Isaac, and with Jacob.
> God saw what was going on with Israel.
> God understood.
>
> EXODUS 2:23 – 25

What a comfort! That gives me the hope that, when I feel like nothing good is happening and I am not seeing visible results for my hard labor, God also listens to my groanings, and he understands.

One day, years after fleeing Egypt, Moses was shepherding the flock of his father-in-law, Jethro. He led the flock to the west end of the wilderness and came to a mountain called Horeb. Suddenly, something wildly supernatural happened.

> The angel of GOD appeared to him in flames of fire blazing out of the middle of a bush. He looked. The bush was blazing away but it didn't burn up.
> Moses said, "What's going on here? I can't believe this! Amazing! Why doesn't the bush burn up?"
> GOD saw that he had stopped to look. God called to him from out of the bush, "Moses! Moses!"
> He said, "Yes? I'm right here!"

God said, "Don't come any closer. Remove your sandals from your feet. You're standing on holy ground."

Then he said, "I am the God of your father: The God of Abraham, the God of Isaac, the God of Jacob."

Moses hid his face, afraid to look at God.

GOD said, "I've taken a good, long look at the affliction of my people in Egypt. I've heard their cries for deliverance from their slave masters; I know all about their pain. And now I have come down to help them, pry them loose from the grip of Egypt, get them out of that country and bring them to a good land with wide-open spaces, a land lush with milk and honey, the land of the Canaanite ...

"I'm sending you to Pharaoh to bring my people, the People of Israel, out of Egypt."

Moses answered God, "But why me? What makes you think that I could ever go to Pharaoh and lead the children of Israel out of Egypt?"

"I'll be with you," God said. "And this will be the proof that I am the one who sent you: When you have brought my people out of Egypt, you will worship God right here at this very mountain."

EXODUS 3:2 – 12

Moses was afraid to face Pharaoh, wondering if the people would believe him or listen to him, and this was God's response:

"Believe me, they will listen to you. Then you and the leaders of Israel will go to the king of Egypt and say to him: 'GOD, the God of the Hebrews, has met with us. Let us take a three-day journey into the wilderness where we will worship GOD — *our* God.'

"I know that the king of Egypt won't let you go unless forced to, so I'll intervene and hit Egypt where it hurts — oh, my miracles will send them reeling! — after which they'll be glad to send you off. I'll see to it that this people get a hearty send-off by the Egyptians — when you leave, you won't leave empty-handed!"

EXODUS 3:18 – 20

Moses felt inadequate to do this huge job, and at the time God appeared to him he didn't yet know the resources God would be providing. But God knew. God provided Moses' brother, Aaron, to help with the speaking part of the mission, and God planned great miracles that would convince people that Moses was empowered by God to do this assignment.

Moses obeyed, God miraculously intervened, and the book of Exodus records the flight of the Israelites from Egypt. At the high points of the story — the pillar of fire protecting the people, the Red Sea parting, and the finger of God carving the Ten Commandments in stone — who would have ever imagined that decades of wandering in the wilderness still lay ahead for the people of God? The result? The people complained against Moses and Aaron while lamenting how they missed the good old days of slavery in Egypt.

Imagine Moses' discouragement as he tried to lead amid all the griping and complaining. What did Moses do? Did he give up and desert the people? Did he take them back to Egypt? No. He persevered. Time and time again, he went back to the Lord with every challenge, and God, demonstrating his infinite mercy, delivered Moses and the people over and over and over again. And Moses repeatedly reminded the people of all God had done. Moses understood that to survive a wilderness experience one must develop the discipline to *remember what the Lord has done.*

So, too, must we. Remember what the Lord has done for us, for others, and for the men and women whose testimonies are recorded in Scripture. When we feel our fires going cold in the wilderness or when we lack the energy to face whatever God has asked us to do, we need to stop and recall what we learned during our own burning bush experiences — to be reminded that we *live* on holy ground.

When God spoke to Moses and others in the Old Testament, they experienced encounters with the holy God. In the New Testament, when Jesus spoke to the disciples, they had an encounter with God. Today, because of the death, burial, and resurrection of Jesus, we have the Holy Spirit indwelling us — and that allows us to have encounters with God daily. Much like a backpacker who carries matches or a tinderbox to provide the spark needed to build a fire in cold, wet, or barren lands, when we encounter discouragement and crises, we can draw on the warmth of the Holy Spirit to rekindle memories of the times when God spoke to our hearts in specific ways. And as we remember what he has done, we find the courage to trust him for an unknown future. I've discovered that when I choose to remain faithful to God — based on his promises, not on what I'm feeling at the moment — that choice allows for the supernatural to take place in my life.

## Document What the Lord Has Done

Looking back, my life has been filled with burning bush experiences, including the birth of my son and the opportunity to direct the Alternative Education Program for Pregnant Teenagers. Then came unwanted moves due to my husband's job transfers to cities where I knew no one, and once again God opened doors and provided opportunities for me to become a director of women's ministries in a large church and for speaking and eventually for writing.

During the wilderness part of those moves, I believed there was nothing good that could come from leaving people and ministries I loved and going to new and frightening places. But as time went on, I remembered what God had done in the past — that wherever we moved he had opened doors, not just for my husband in new jobs, but also for me through God-given opportunities to use my gifts of Bible teaching and mentoring and to be stretched in new, exciting ways that were far better than what I had left behind. I didn't always see those results immediately, but I could be confident they would come because of my remembrance of what God had done in the past.

I don't believe it comes naturally to any of us to remember what the Lord has done. What *does* come naturally? Complaining about our "now," just as the Israelites did. But such complaining douses the fires of our faith at our lowest points, just when we need to be building and nurturing our wildfire faith. If our goal is to grow a wildfire faith that endures, then we must practice remembering what the Lord has done.

Here's a tool you can use — one I've found very helpful over the years. Before reading the next section, take a moment to reflect on and document your own burning bush experiences. At the top of the page write, "Remember What the Lord Has Done." Date your experiences and record the type of wilderness you were in. Identify how God spoke to you — through his Word, through other people, through specific books or teachings from

Christian leaders, or through opportunities that opened up—and then document what happened as a result.

Then save that list. You are going to need it in your next wilderness experience. I know I did.

## A Different Kind of Wilderness

We had just passed the thirteenth year of Jason's incarceration when I received an unexpected invitation to speak at the prison where he is a resident. It's unusual to be allowed to be a volunteer speaker within a prison where you have a relative. I knew this opportunity represented great favor, and I immediately said I would come.

In truth, I had been struggling with the length of Jason's sentence—endless. As we have discussed, there is an ebb and flow to our spiritual lives, and at the time I was living off the embers of my faith rather than a brightly lit, well-fueled spiritual fire. Yet, I could not resist the obvious open door of ministering to many of the men I knew from my visits to the prison. These inmates make up our church family at what we call "Church of the Razor Wire," where Gene and I spend each Sunday when we are not involved in out-of-state ministry. We connect with our inmate brothers in Christ in the visitation room.

Gene and I drove to the prison together, met the officers in charge, passed through security, and entered the large meeting area. The inmates were already seated and were enthusiastic and respectful as I shared our journey of receiving a middle-of-the-night phone call that forever changed our lives. Several prison officials joined us, and they, too, listened carefully to my message.

Halfway through the presentation I asked Gene to come up

and talk to the men about a father's tears. With great tenderness and honest emotion Gene shared his own testimony:

> Carol and I are honored to be with you today. We see many of you here on the weekends when you are visiting with your families, and we feel privileged to call you our friends. I grew up in a home where my parents sent me to church on Sundays, but they didn't attend themselves. Then one day a new pastor in our town came to visit, and he shared the gospel with my mother and dad and with me, and I invited Jesus Christ into my life. I didn't know what the future would hold, but I eventually married that preacher's daughter.

The men chuckled and looked in my direction. Some elbowed our son. Gene went on.

> Five years after I married Carol, Jason was born. I had tears of joy. I was a new dad, and I could hardly believe that God had given me a son. As Jason grew up, he became my running buddy. We did a half marathon together, and I discovered I am definitely "the old guy" compared to his energy and strength, but those were great times of bonding as a father and son.

I noticed a few of the inmates wiping away tears, which surprised me.

> My son and I often read the same books so we could discuss them together. We both enjoyed science fiction, adventuresome military novels, and challenging books on spiritual development. When Jason graduated from high school, I was a proud father — especially when my

son received an appointment to the U.S. Naval Academy. I remember those four exciting years and the tears of happiness when he graduated and the midshipmen tossed their hats into the air. I wondered what the future would hold for my son, and I was sure it would be good.

As I viewed the group from where I sat, I wondered what the inmates were thinking about their own relationships with their fathers.

I remember tears of joy when Jason fell in love and married the woman of his dreams. One year passed, and I knew my son had been troubled about the possibility that the biological father of his two stepdaughters was about to get unsupervised visitation with the girls. With hearing multiple allegations of abuse against that man, Jason was anxious. However, nothing prepared me for the call telling me that my son had shot and killed this man and that he had been arrested for first-degree murder. My tears of sorrow for the family of the deceased, as well as for the multiple losses of my son and his family, have at times overwhelmed me.

This was not on our agenda for our own lives or for our son's life, and we are not ashamed to tell you that we do not apologize for our tears. But we also want you to know we have hope, because the God who was faithful to us before our son's arrest is the same God who is giving us hope for a better future — if not here on earth, then in heaven where all of us who know him personally will walk in freedom.

Gene gave the microphone back to me. I told the inmates that statistics tell us only 6 percent of them had loving fathers and that my heart ached for all they had experienced, but I reminded them that they could each be the first person in their family to change future generations. I began to hear the sound of weeping as the presence of the Holy Spirit continued to move in hearts. At the end, I challenged them to do four things:

1. Get to know Jesus personally.
2. Write out a gratitude list of everything you have to be thankful for.
3. Write to your children, even if you never hear from them.
4. Do one act of kindness for someone on the prison compound every day.

As I prayed for them, grown men were sobbing, and one man on the front row had moved from his chair to his knees, crying out to God. The Spirit of the Lord was palpable in that place. Instantly, I recognized that the Holy Spirit had invaded this man's life, and I felt honored to see it with my own eyes. A flush of awe washed over me as I fought back fresh tears of my own. I connected with the men in that room as if they were my own sons and brothers. For a few minutes, God allowed me to experience the weight of the bleak, harsh, desperate environment they live in, but I also experienced the audacious light that only comes when the Spirit of God pierces the darkness. A lump rose in my throat as I again processed reality: "This is where my son lives."

On the way home I marveled over this burning bush experience — a marker moment of knowing that, although my life as the mother of an inmate would never be easy, God was revealing that he was opening doors for a ministry I had not anticipated. I knew I could choose to stay stuck in a wilderness of hopelessness, or I could recognize the Holy Spirit's saying, "This is the way; walk in it" (Isaiah 30:21 NIV).

Think back to Moses as he received the commandments up on the mountain just when the Israelites were at their worst, and how that experience equipped him to face the next forty years in the wilderness. We all have moments when we run dry and must lean on memories of God's faithfulness rather than on our current circumstances, when we must rely on our knowledge of God's Spirit at work in the past to keep our fire going in the present.

This unexpected experience of ministry in my son's prison — at a time when my own faith seemed in slow burn rather than vibrant flame — became for me a startling burning bush moment. Like the experience with the girls in Project 23, it was a case of God showing up and invading this earth with his power, not me generating some brilliant spiritual plan. My part was simply to show up and be available. My reward was a front-row seat, watching God transform lives.

## My Father's Perspective

My daddy recently passed into the arms of Jesus. Jason was his firstborn grandchild. Soon after our son's conviction and life sentence, my father visited Jason in prison. As he walked out of the prison by my side, Dad said to me, "I wish I could trade places with him. I'm an old man, and Jason has his whole life ahead of him. But I know God is using him in a powerful way. That young man isn't just surviving; he's thriving!"

My father was right. Thanks to his many years of walking with the Lord, he could see the eternal value of what God, our heavenly Father, was accomplishing in and through Jason's life.

It was Daddy's life of faith that first sparked Gene's life of faith when Gene was just a teenager. Surely the salvation of young Gene was a burning bush moment in my dad's life.

Gene stood in the prison and shared one of his own burning bush moments with the inmates gathered that day — the day his son was born — and he spoke of his confidence that the God who was faithful to us before our son's arrest is the same God who is giving us hope for a better future — if not here on earth, then in heaven where all of us who know him personally will walk in freedom. That testimony became a burning bush moment for inmates who turned to God that day.

Jason lives every day within prison walls. How easy it would be to lose sight of God's eternal purposes and to wallow in self-pity and despair. But he remembers what God has done in the past, and it gives him the momentum to look to a future that is filled with hope and joy.

I've seen the *shekinah* glory of God inside the prison. I have experienced what the light of Jesus does to a person who embraces his truth, and those memories — those burning bush moments — help keep me determined to live out a radically faith-filled life.

I love the burning bush moments when God is so close I hear him speaking to me, but I also know that wherever I am, God is present with me, indwelling me with his Holy Spirit. This means that even when that burning bush is out of sight, God is just as present through his Word, through his people when I fellowship with them, through the stories of his presence in my life, and through the testimonies of others.

I challenged you earlier in this chapter to document what the Lord has done in your life. Remember all that God has done for his people and for you. Celebrate that list and revisit it to recall your own burning bush moments. Use it as a reminder that you are standing on holy ground so that the memories of all that God has done in your life will fuel a wildfire faith that will endure anything.

## COME TO THE FIRE

1. Carol talks about several of her own burning bush experiences — times when God revealed himself to her in specific ways or through unique opportunities. Describe one of the most important or memorable burning bush moments you've experienced in your relationship with God. What was it about this experience that you would describe as "holy ground"?

2. Moses felt totally inadequate to do the huge job God put in his lap — to lead the people of Israel out of Egypt. Has there been a time in your life when you felt God was asking you to do something for him that was way out of your comfort zone? What happened? If you said yes, how did God meet your needs?

3. James wrote, "You know that when your faith is tested, your endurance has a chance to grow. So let it grow, for when your endurance is fully developed, you will be perfect and complete, needing nothing" (James 1:3–4 NLT). What do you think "so let it grow" means? What implications might this Scripture passage have for you in your current circumstances?

## FIRE-BUILDING CHALLENGE

Earlier in this chapter, you were asked to remember what the Lord has done by identifying the type of wilderness you were in and by writing out how God spoke to you — through his Word, through other people, through books or teachings from Christian leaders, or through opportunities that opened up. Pick one of those experiences and share it with someone this week. Be creative. You might share your experience in person, by telephone, in an e-mail, or in a blog — in your small group or with a friend.

# CHAPTER 5

# The Spark

As Jesus was walking along, he saw a man
named Matthew sitting at his tax collector's booth.
"Follow me and be my disciple," Jesus said to him.
So Matthew got up and followed him.

**Matthew 9:9 NLT**

It was an ordinary Sunday morning. Our family of seven had just returned home from church, and we piled out of the car and into the kitchen through the screen door on the side of the house. Dad came in last, and he was weeping. I had never seen him cry before, and it startled me. Turning to my mother, he blurted out, "I'm either going to have to get out of church work completely or comply with God's will and go into the ministry."

Then Mama started crying, and I had no idea what was going on. But our pastor had begun a series of sermons on Jonah — the prophet who initially responded to God's call by heading in the wrong direction — and my dad was miserable. Now, as the oldest of five children, I observed what happened over the next few weeks from my thirteen-year-old perspective. Before I was born, my father believed God was leading him into the ministry and he went to Bible college, but when the financial pressures of providing for a young family hit, he left school and went into the insurance business. One by one, more children arrived, and then he had a large family to feed. Now compelled by God to enter the ministry, he went to see his boss, a man who didn't know the Lord, and said, "I realize agents in this business are full-time employees, but God has called me to preach. Would it be possible for me to work part-time to care for my family while I go to Bible school?"

The man leaned back in his chair, scratched his head, and said, "Well, Clyde, as long as your sales keep up, you'll get your full paycheck. We'll just see what happens."

When Dad got home and told that story, reality struck. I would become a preacher's kid. It wasn't a role I was looking forward to. I watched as my father went to school during the day and sold insurance in the evenings. Many nights he came through the door and said, "Pauline, tonight I sold an eternal life insurance policy too. It was a thrill to share the gospel with this young couple." Mama rejoiced. The energy and excitement my parents expressed about their joy in seeing people come to faith ignited something in my heart. I felt an undeniable desire to be part of something big — something so rewarding it would be worth any sacrifice. I wanted to share my faith too. I longed to do something significant with the energy and resources I had, but I had no idea what that would look like.

I also witnessed my parents choosing to forgo a nicer house, a newer vehicle, and a more affluent lifestyle to pursue full-time ministry. I knew my father's paycheck was based on whether or not he sold enough insurance to earn his salary — and month by month, during the entire time Dad was completing his education, his sales were higher than they had ever been. As their response to God's call unfolded, I saw how my parents' passionate faith paved the way for an unknown but exciting future in full-time ministry.

I also recognized their fears. In fact, I shared them. How would God provide for our big family if Dad left his job? Would we be lonely if we left West Michigan and moved to a place where we had no extended family and no friends? Would people think my father was irrational for making such a life-altering, drastic change in his late thirties? Was this the voice of adventure calling? Or was it definitely the voice of God? Yet, in the face of those fears I watched my parents leap into the future, willing to take every risk in obedience to God's call. And their leap planted a tiny spark of desire in me to do the same.

## Every Fire Begins with a Spark

Sparks are powerful. When I was a child, Smokey the Bear made public service announcements on television, warning, "Only *you* can prevent forest fires." From Smokey I learned to never be careless with campfires. One tiny spark could easily ignite some dry tinder that might result in thousands of acres lost to a forest fire. Massive wildfires from one small spark.

Perhaps one of the most beautiful mysteries of wildfire faith is how it begins and spreads. Like fire, there is a wondrous cycle of one spark leading to a flaming fire that ignites yet another new fire. The spark that ignited my faith found a heart of dry tinder ready for flame when I was just five years old.

My mother had the radio on, and while playing by her side I began listening to a drama about a man whose life was transformed by Jesus Christ. He talked about the sin of his past and the joy of having his burden lifted, and about discovering there was a better way to live. That day the Holy Spirit's gentle whisper said, "Come," and I said, "Yes."

Mama guided me through Scripture and knelt beside me as I, too, confessed my sin and asked Jesus to come into my heart. As a strong-willed child, I knew I was a sinner who needed forgiveness. That incident was the spark that grew over the years into a flame of passion within me — a passion to do something that would outlast my life and provide a meaningful answer to the question, "When my life is over, will it matter that I was here?"

When the flames of my faith first flickered into life, I had no idea what the future would hold. How could a five-year-old anticipate the unthinkable pain I would encounter as an adult, that there would be days when I would discover that, even for a Christian, life can be very difficult? All I knew was that I had said yes to Jesus. My sins were forgiven and I felt the warmth of his presence in my life. I was drawn to the God of the flame. My faith was far from mature, but I knew beyond any doubt that God was real and that he loved me.

I was fourteen when Dad finished his Bible school education and became the pastor of a little church on the south end of a small town in Michigan called Durand. Oak Street Church was a small, struggling body of believers, and they had asked my father if he would lead them. Mom and Dad purchased a house in the community and thrust themselves into the task of growing a church.

There were forty-two people in the congregation on the first Sunday — and seven of them were in our family. I had four years of piano lessons under my belt, so I became the church pianist. We sang slow hymns for one very good reason — I couldn't play any faster! And it helped when the songs were in the key of B flat. I could "plunk-thud" on the keyboard in that key, so it sounded more like music than a "joyful noise."

Mom and Dad made a lot of house calls during the first few months, visiting and sharing their faith with people who had attended a church service. I was the chief babysitter for my four younger siblings, and I had a sense of mission connected with this unsalaried job. I knew my work made it possible for Mom and Dad to spread the fire of God's truth in our community, and even as a young teenager I realized that my willingness to participate allowed me to be part of a mission bigger than I could have imagined.

Watching my parents choose a life of ministry was a major factor in building my young faith. Because they talked to me about the challenges and opportunities to touch lives with God's truth, I was eager to participate by using my gifts of praying, playing the piano, and babysitting to contribute to an important cause. The truth of Paul's statement to Timothy inspired me:

> That precious memory triggers another: your honest faith — and what a rich faith it is, handed down ... to you! And the special gift of ministry you received ... keep that ablaze! God doesn't want us to be shy with his gifts, but bold and loving and sensible.
>
> 2 TIMOTHY 1:5 – 7

## The Funeral, the Alcoholic, and the Preacher

I'm sure my father never dreamed that one of his first responsibilities as a full-time pastor would be to officiate the funeral of a five-year-old child.

It was the first day of kindergarten, and Cindy was wearing a pair of brand-new patent leather shoes. As she looked down at her shoes while crossing the street, Cindy never saw the car that hit her. In a moment, her life was gone.

Dad was asked to speak at her funeral service. Cindy had naturally curly hair that hung in pretty blonde ringlets around her face. Mama said later, "In that stark white coffin, she looked like a porcelain doll. Too young. Too much life ahead of her. Too soon."

Ace Spencer came to the funeral drunk. Cindy was his niece, the daughter of his brother. Ace loved this little girl and was deeply distraught by her death. In the lobby, family members told him the new preacher in town was speaking at the service and that he was also calling on folks in the area. Upon meeting Dad, Ace looked up and with slurred speech muttered, "Well, Preacher, when you gonna come and visit me?" Later, Dad made the appointment, and Mother and Dad went to Ace's home.

Dad's description of Ace was poignant: "He was a drunk, a wife beater, and he wouldn't even have had a house to live in apart from the grace of his father-in-law. Ace drank up his money, and his father-in-law routinely brought groceries to the house for his daughter, Sheri, and their three children."

My parents shared Christ with Ace and Sheri on that visit, but neither one was ready to take the first step of faith. Another time, Dad visited Ace in the hospital, where he was drying out from a drinking spree. Ace still wasn't buying into the gospel, but he liked Dad, and the Spirit of God was working in his heart. Ace was released from the hospital a few days later and went home.

The Spencers had an old television that could only get, at most, three channels. The only channel that came in that week was airing a Billy Graham crusade. Ace was beyond irritated. But he had nothing else to watch, so for three nights in a row he tuned in — and God used Billy Graham to prepare him for a visit from Mom and Dad the next evening. That night, after they heard the gospel once again, Ace and Sheri both invited Jesus Christ into their lives.

As Ace walked Mom and Dad to the front door, he asked, "How much do I owe you, Preacher?" He was sure something so wonderful must come with a price tag.

Dad smiled as he put his arm around Ace's shoulders. "You don't owe me anything, Ace. It's free."

When my parents returned home and told the story of Ace and Sheri's coming to faith in Christ, my heart leaped. Mom and Dad put their arms around me, thanked me for participating in the ministry by caring for the younger children, and we had a celebration prayer together. The Holy Spirit was breathing oxygen into the small fire in my soul, blessing me with the warmth and light of his presence and with the immeasurable joy that comes when God is at work in people's lives. I was beginning to experience the delight of watching the spark of faith come alive in other people, and I longed for God to use me to help others investigate who Jesus is.

Do you see the power of sparks in the life of faith? We never know what act of obedience, what relationship that crosses our path, or what circumstance might lead to a spark of faith leaping from the life of a believer into the heart of a nonbeliever. But once we grasp the power of sparks, we begin to live in expectancy with eyes wide open, watching for the sparks that God carries into new lives on the wind of his Spirit.

## Another Spark Ignited

Three years after we arrived in the railroad town of Durand, Michigan, Mom and Dad had a surprise — child number six, who was also daughter number five. The child born five years earlier was our only brother, Ben — redheaded, freckle faced, and born on Halloween, with a disposition to match. Now we had a new baby girl, and her name was Joy. My name is Carol Joy, so I felt a special closeness to this sister who was given part of my name.

However, with a new baby in the house, the job of caring for my now *five* younger siblings was more challenging. It was New Year's Day, my holiday off from school, and my father asked if I would watch the kids while he and Mother made a call on the Kent family. Dad had met a man named Francis Kent in the hospital a few weeks earlier and sensed a spiritual hunger in his heart. I grudgingly told Dad I would take care of the children, and my parents drove to the home of the Kent family.

Mr. and Mrs. Kent invited them to have coffee at the kitchen table. Dad had his Bible with him, and after getting to know them more personally, he briefly shared the gospel message: "God loves you. He sent his Son, Jesus, to be the Savior of the world. He longs for a personal relationship with you." After a few moments, he asked Mr. and Mrs. Kent if they would like to pray a simple prayer inviting Christ into their lives.

Suddenly, a voice came from the doorway between the kitchen and the living room. Gene, the couple's teenage son, spoke up and said, "I've been listening in on this conversation, and I wondered, 'Could I become a Christian too?'"

Gene joined his parents, and all three of them, with my mother and dad at their sides, got on their knees around the kitchen table and said yes to Jesus. When Mom and Dad got home and shared that story, I was beyond excited.

Dad had rules, and one of them was, "There will be no dating of non-Christians for my five daughters." At that time, there were eight girls in our church youth group and two guys, and neither of the guys had caught my interest. I couldn't believe there was now a third candidate in the form of handsome, dynamic Gene Kent.

Are you ahead of me on this story? That day while I was home doing the mundane, ordinary, not-very-much-loved job of babysitting, my mother and father were out winning my future husband to Jesus Christ. The spark of faith took root in Gene Kent, and not too much later he asked me out on our first date, and a few more sparks (of a different nature) flew! Gene Kent's life would never be the same, not because he started dating me, but because he began falling in love with Jesus.

## With Jesus at the Fire

Sparks can do more than simply start new fires; they can also rekindle dying fires. Have you ever blown on a waning fire, sending sparks flying that in turn reignited the fire? I believe that is exactly what Jesus was doing that morning on the beach in Galilee (John 21).

It's postresurrection, and Jesus is about to make a surprise appearance on the shore of the Sea of Galilee. The seven disciples are out in a boat, and they have had a rough night. When Simon Peter announced he was going fishing, the other six decided to join him. But they have caught nothing — after working *all night*. Discouraging, to say the least!

Now Jesus is standing on the beach at the crack of dawn, but the disciples don't recognize him. Keep in mind, just days before they had experienced the agonizing and frightening scene of Jesus' crucifixion and death, followed by their amazing encounter with the risen Lord. No wonder they don't recognize him.

Jesus calls out, "Fellows, have you caught any fish?" They give their disappointing answer — no fish are biting. Then Jesus says, "Throw out your net on the right-hand side of the boat, and you'll get some!" So they do, and then they can't haul the net into the boat because there are so many fish in it.

John speaks to Peter: "It's the Lord!" When Simon Peter realizes it is the Master, he puts on his tunic, dives into the water, and heads directly to shore. The others follow in the boat, pulling the loaded net behind them. When all seven are on solid ground, they discover that Jesus has made a campfire and that breakfast is waiting for them — fish cooking over the fire and also bread.

Pause for a moment and think about Peter. When he realized it was Jesus on the shore, he responded instantly. The sound of his Master's voice ignited within him a desire to be with Jesus as soon as possible. I love the spontaneity of that scene!

Jesus tells them to bring some of the fish they've caught, and Peter drags the net to shore. There were 153 large fish, but the net wasn't broken. Then he invites them to have some breakfast. I can only imagine their joy in sharing a meal with Jesus, their teacher, friend, and miracle-working Lord brought back from the dead. They were having their own private "come to the fire" experience, being fed not only with fresh fish but with words from the Son of God. Jesus was reigniting their flames of faith, restoring their spiritual fire. In this act of love, I see Jesus showering fresh sparks on the faith of his disciples in at least three ways.

*1. Jesus anticipated their needs.* I tend to be the most discouraged when I'm tired and hungry, so this is a noteworthy example of Jesus caring for our physical needs as well as our spiritual ones. In your own life, think of ways in which God meets your physical needs. How does he provide nourishment and rest? Have you ever thought of his care as sparks from his fire to yours? He sends countless sparks into our lives that we never even notice. Notice them! Your faith will grow for it.

*2. Jesus reaffirmed his personal relationship with them.* Likewise, when I "come to the fire" of God's truth through spending time with him, I experience a connection with the lover of my soul, and I feel significant to the One from whom I want affirmation. You, too, can share in that fellowship with Jesus through prayer, his Word, and worship.

It is the next act of Jesus, however, that opens my eyes to an entirely new perspective on how sparks can feed our fire.

*3. Jesus called Peter to feed his lambs.* Following the meal, Jesus focuses his attention on Peter, asking him three times, "Do you love me?" Peter's answers were direct and simple: "Yes, Master, you know I love you." Jesus then challenges Peter to feed his lambs and to take care of his sheep. The very act of caring for God's people, of meeting their needs in acts of service, generates sparks to feed our own wildfires and also sends sparks flying into the lives of others.

## We Never Know Which Spark Becomes a Wildfire

Remember the story about the alcoholic my mother and dad led to Jesus? When Ace Spencer came to faith in Christ, his life took a 180-degree turn. He started treating his wife, Sheri, with respect. With her help, he memorized John 3:16 and began carrying his Bible to work, even though he was illiterate.

Ace worked at the Buick Motor Company in Flint, Michigan,

and his cronies were bikers and drinking buddies. He would often sit during his lunch breaks with an open Bible in his lap. His heart burned with a desire to share his faith with his coworkers, and he prayed, "God, if you want me to talk to these guys about you, you'll have to send them over here."

One by one, the men came by to talk. They realized what Ace had experienced was *real* — and he didn't need to stand on a soapbox and preach. He became God's spark in that factory and eventually led over two hundred men to Christ. The flame of faith spread like wildfire!

One weekend several years later, my father was ministering in a church where he heard a missionary from Brazil named Gordon recount his testimony. Gordon spoke of how he had blatantly rejected God and was adamantly opposed to the gospel. But his sister and her husband lived in Flint and his brother-in-law worked at Buick Motor Company.

Gordon told how a coworker had witnessed to his brother-in-law and led him to Christ. In turn, his brother-in-law's wife came to faith. They began to pray for Gordon. Four years later, God answered their prayers. Gordon and his wife gave their lives to Christ, accepted the call to missions, and to this day serve God in Brazil. And who was that coworker? You've already guessed the answer: Ace Spencer.

The epigraph at the beginning of this chapter tells of Jesus' call to Matthew to follow him. Matthew was at the tax collector's booth. He may have been skimming off the top, gathering a bit of extra income for himself, doing what other tax collectors did at that time in history. When Jesus passed by, he didn't just see what Matthew's life was at that moment; he looked at him with eyes that could foresee all the potential Matthew had for becoming one of the biographers of Jesus' life.

Jesus said, "Follow me and be my disciple." And Matthew did. The spark ignited, and Matthew's life was forever changed. When God looks at you, he doesn't just see your less-than-perfect choices or your current struggles and honest doubts; he sees in you all the potential of becoming a Christ follower who shares the spark of his hope, life, and joy with everyone you meet.

Two simple practices can help you make the most of every spark to keep your wildfire faith going strong.

1. *See the spark.* In this chapter, we've marveled at the mystery of how tiny sparks can take root and begin fresh fires in the most unexpected places. Take a few minutes now to trace the origin of the spark that ignited your flame. Where did it come from? Whose faith reached into your life? Who inspired the faith of that person? And whose fire threw that spark? See how far back you can trace the spark, and celebrate God's mysterious ways. Only then can you catch a vision for the next practice.

2. *Be the spark.* As you share your faith — through the words you speak, acts of service you offer, obedient responses you make to God's call — it will spark new wildfires in the lives of others. Sometimes, as with my daddy and my husband, we will see the immediate and direct results of our spark igniting faith in the life of another. And sometimes, as in the case of Ace and Gordon, we may not see the results for many years. Ace learned much later that one spark from his faith traveled through another into the heart of a man God then called to be a missionary to Brazil.

See the spark. Be the spark. As you do, you will join countless believers whose wildfire faith continues to spread over all the earth.

## COME TO THE FIRE

1. What was the first spark of faith in you? What caused that spark, and when did it begin?
2. Carol told the story of watching her parents give up a higher standard of living to follow God's leading and go into the ministry. Their example impacted her greatly. Who made a deep impression on your life that became a model for growing a passionate relationship with Christ?
3. The apostle Paul believed in encouraging the spark of faith in those who were younger than him — chronologically or spiritually (see 2 Timothy 1:5 – 7). Is there someone in your life you are mentoring in his or her faith walk? If so, has the journey been encouraging and fulfilling, or challenging and difficult?
4. In the story about Jesus and the disciples in John 21, we learn about how the men had fished all night without results. But that didn't mean they didn't know how to fish. Have you ever shared your faith — with no results? How did that experience impact your intimacy with God? Have you experienced the opportunity of leading someone to Christ? Describe what happened.

## FIRE-BUILDING CHALLENGE

During the breakfast meal shared by Jesus and his disciples around the campfire, Jesus told Peter to feed his sheep. Take a few moments to record ways you have cared for the practical needs of God's people. Are you actively engaged in such service now? If not, commit to pray for God's leading in this area so that you, too, can spark the faith of others through acts of service.

CHAPTER 6

# Tending the Fire

It takes time to come to the fire, it takes effort to keep the
fire burning, it takes a willingness to become quiet enough
to hear what God might be saying, and it takes courage to
snuff out competing sounds and demands that attempt to
shorten or neutralize the effect of the fire time.

Gail MacDonald, *High Call, High Privilege*

My heart was aching with disappointment and sadness. Our
daughter-in-law came to us in the summer of 2005 and said,
"I need to give the girls a more stable life. It isn't normal for
little girls to spend every weekend in the visitation area of a
maximum-security prison. They need soccer on Saturdays, and
they need church on Sundays." I felt emotion rise up within me,
and my heart raced. Gene held my hand tightly. She went on.
"I've decided to move out of state, and if I separate from Jason,
I will no longer be in touch with you."

I could hardly breathe. I knew it had been a difficult six
and a half years for all of us, but especially for Jason's wife.
Chelsea and Hannah were only six and three when we first
met them, and now they were thirteen and ten. Within two
months of this conversation, our daughter-in-law had packed

up and moved out of state with the girls. Jason is our only child, and Chelsea and Hannah are our only grandchildren. I felt the agony of my son as he realized his wife and stepdaughters were leaving him, and it multiplied my own grief.

They left in the fall of that same year, and we understood why. Only a year earlier, four major hurricanes had hit Florida, and three of them ripped through the center of the state, causing massive damage to our daughter-in-law's home. She had already endured the murder, the years of waiting for a trial, the conviction, and her husband's incarceration — now this! There was roof damage, and the wallboard was warping from the massive rainfall that was followed by the intense heat of the sun. Mold settled into the carpets, the closets, and even the drawers. It was difficult to find contractors to make repairs because there was colossal damage all over the state.

The storm left a damaged home, but it also brought about a sense of hopelessness. Something in our daughter-in-law's spirit seemed to break. She was ready to move on. In spite of our own hurt and sadness, we understood her desire to make a new beginning somewhere else.

In the aftermath of Jason's trial and conviction, Gene and I had relocated from Michigan to Florida to be near Jason and his family. Relationships that go untended don't survive, and we wanted to keep our family relationships strong and healthy. I had taken some comfort in knowing that at least my son would be able to see his family at weekend visitations and that we would be nearby to help our daughter-in-law with the inevitable hardships that come with an incarcerated spouse. I thought we would finally be able to find a new kind of normal and learn how to function in the aftermath of this devastating crisis. But now our granddaughters were gone from our lives.

As Gene and I dealt with the loss of our granddaughters, there were sore spots — topics that would trigger pain. We had intentionally purchased a home with a pool in the backyard because our granddaughters loved to swim; we knew it would provide wonderful opportunities for them to have exercise and fun when they came for visits. But they left Florida before they had even one opportunity to swim in that pool. I wondered why God opened the door for a larger home than we needed if our grandgirls were not going to live near us. Every time I looked at that pool, a knife twisted inside me.

Six and a half years passed, and during that time we sent birthday gifts, Christmas gifts, food items, financial help, cards, and special occasion paper goods for celebrating holidays. We wanted the girls to know we were praying for them to find new friends and that we loved them dearly. Even though we thought we had a correct postal box number, we never knew for sure that our gifts were received. I took delight in wrapping each package with tender loving care — in colorful paper and lacy ribbons in the girls' favorite pastels. I thought that would make them smile. The gifts were the only way we could find to tend and care for our relationship with our granddaughters, and they were always sent with many prayers, and sometimes a few tears.

During this long absence, my prayer life was intensely focused on the girls — that God would protect them, that he would link them with Christians who would encourage them and provide friendship and companionship. I prayed for their academic success and that they would not have scars from the deep trauma they had gone through during their growing-up years. I prayed they would grow in their faith and be drawn to God's truth. I also prayed they would know how much Gene and I loved them and longed to have them back in our lives.

Then came the summer of 2011. It was late August, and I was in Dallas at a Bible software training conference. My author-friend Kendra Smiley was also attending the conference, and we happened to be seated together on a van ride to the venue. She inquired about Jason and asked for an update on any new developments. Kendra provided a safe place for me to spill out my heart. And I did.

"Kendra, for the past six and a half years, Gene and I have sent gifts, cards, and tangible encouragement to the girls. We never know if our gifts are received, and we've never gotten any kind of a note or call from them in all this time. They are now nineteen and sixteen. They're becoming adults. At what point should Gene and I stop sending gifts? I really don't want to be stalker grandparents if they don't want us in their lives."

Without a moment's hesitation, Kendra looked into my eyes and said, "Carol, don't *ever* stop. As long as those gifts are not returned, those girls will know how much you and Gene love them. Never put an end date on sending them all of that encouragement."

My faith was weak, but I trusted Kendra's advice. We would continue to tend our relationships with the girls, even without knowing if it mattered to them at all. That was August. Just one month later, I was speaking at Malone University in Canton, Ohio. On the way home, Gene and I had a layover at the Atlanta airport. I was planning to stay in the area to spend a few days with friends, and Gene was heading home to Florida. We had lunch together at the airport before saying our goodbyes. Thirty minutes later, Gene was at the gate waiting for his connecting flight. I was in another area where I would soon be gathering with my friends before traveling to our "girlfriends' getaway" location.

My cell phone rang. It was Gene. When we're away, our home phone is forwarded to Gene's cell phone. His voice was breathless. With great emotion he said, "Carol, I just got off the phone with Chelsea. This tiny, soft-spoken voice said, 'Grampy, it's Chelsea. I'm nineteen years old, and I'm a freshman in college, and I miss my family.'"

I could hear the emotion in Gene's voice, and I was weeping with joy. Chelsea was in a university far from where we lived, so we couldn't see each other immediately. Soon after this call, however, the three of us made an appointment to Skype, and we saw our precious Chelsea on the computer screen — all grown-up. She was so full of love and tenderness and joy at renewing our relationship. Our hearts leaped for joy.

She flew to Florida for Thanksgiving weekend and had a reunion with her dad at the prison. Her hands were ice-cold as she went through security, and I knew she was full of apprehension, but it didn't take long for the conversation to explode with memories and updates and laughter and tears. It was a very special reunion, and I watched the joy flood over my son as God answered his prayers for a reunion with his daughter.

Chelsea came for a month during her Christmas vacation from university studies and then again for ten days over spring break. During each visit, she was reintroduced to relatives she hadn't seen in more than six years, and she and her dad had multiple opportunities to grow in their relationship.

By this time, we'd had a couple of delightful occasions to connect with Hannah via Skype, and we marveled at her quick wit and at how grown-up she was. During Chelsea's spring break, Hannah said, "Gramps and Grams, when I graduate from high school in June, may I come to Florida with Chelsea and spend the summer with you too?" God opened every door for Hannah and Chelsea to spend the summer with us, and during that time Hannah also had multiple visits with her dad.

Jason's joy at being reunited with his girls is beyond description. It's complicated because he longs to be actively involved in parenting on a day-to-day basis, and there are great limitations because of his incarceration. He's limited to fifteen-minute phone calls that are automatically cut off when the time is up, and meeting in a public visitation room doesn't provide the kind of intimate setting for the in-depth talks he would like to have with his girls. But God has brought about renewed relationships, and we rejoice in that!

Jason and his wife are still officially married, but they have not seen each other in over six years. We understand the pain of her journey and the ache in her soul, and she is always in our prayers.

## Time Well Spent

No fire can continue burning without being fed and tended. Whether it's a relationship with a friend, a family member, or God, intimacy takes time. We do this when we take time to talk, listen, and do enjoyable things together. When Gene and I spend time together, we take walks, share funny stories, and exchange ideas; we discuss our fears, celebrate our successes, and plan our vacations — because that will mean we have uninterrupted time to spend together. The more we are together, the closer we get, but the more we are apart, the more distant we feel. With our granddaughters, we close that distance with calls, Skype, e-mail, Facebook, and, as often as feasible, face-to-face visits. All these are examples of what it means to tend a relationship.

My friend Tammie said, "I've come to see that spiritual passion is much like a marriage relationship. As in any relationship, there are moments of great desire and emotion that spur us on. And there are those times when faith is a quiet comfort — peaceful, easy, known. The secret of living in the warmth of the fire is in doing life side by side. I yearn to experience all of life with Christ as my partner." The truth: Tending the fire of our faith requires spending time with God.

No matter how busy Jesus was, he spent time alone with his Father. The first chapter in Mark's gospel offers a fascinating glimpse of twenty-four hours in the life of Christ (Mark 1:21 – 35). How did he spend his time? He was in Capernaum and began that Sabbath day by preaching in the synagogue. While he was speaking, a demon-possessed man caused a disruption. Jesus spoke with authority and drove out the evil spirit, amazing the crowd that had never seen anything like this before.

After leaving the synagogue, he went with James and John to the home of Simon and Andrew, where he healed Simon's mother-in-law of a fever. That same day, after sunset, people brought their sick and demon-possessed friends and relatives to Jesus. In fact, "the whole city lined up at his door!" (Mark 1:33).

I get out of breath just thinking about what Jesus was doing that day — preaching, driving out demons, traveling to the home of Simon and Andrew (while talking to James and John), healing Simon's mother-in-law, and ministering to the many who showed up on the doorstep. At that point I would have closed the blinds and turned out my lights, hoping no one else would ring my doorbell. Not Jesus. He walked out the door and "cured their sick bodies and tormented spirits" (Mark 1:34).

Following a day like that, I wouldn't have been surprised if

Jesus took the next few days off, but he didn't. "While it was still night, way before dawn, he got up and went out to a secluded spot and prayed" (Mark 1:35). After the busiest day in the recorded history of his ministry, Jesus got up early so he could enjoy the presence of his Father. The example of Jesus getting refueled for life and ministry in the middle of a chaotic schedule by spending intimate time with his Father reminds me that I can never use busyness as a reason to skip the warmth of the fire — time in God's Word, listening, learning, hanging out together.

Marlae Gritter is the executive vice president of Moms in Prayer International. I first met Marlae when she was a mother to young children and realized how desperately she needed to spend time in prayer — to grow in personal spiritual vibrancy and to pray for her children. God used her in a profound way to influence my prayer life. She suggested that women plan for an occasional "DAWG day" (Day Alone with God). She describes it as "a specific day when you plan ahead to spend time alone with God. The location might be in your own home or at a park, library, or retreat center."

She explains that the structure can vary: Bible study; prayer; listening to what God says to your heart; singing or worshiping; reading a chapter of an inspiring biography or a book on spiritual discipline or Christian leadership. Marlae suggests that if you have young children, good friends can trade childcare responsibilities to free each other for the opportunity to enjoy God in solitude. These days can be renewing, spiritually challenging, and essential for growing a love relationship with Jesus. If you don't have a full day because of work responsibilities, plan for a half day or for two hours of time when you cut yourself loose from social media, e-mail, and your cell phone — and you listen to God's voice.

The important thing, no matter your stage of life, is to make a plan for spending time with God. Tending your relationship with God is a top priority for keeping your wildfire faith alive and growing.

## Lessons from My Son

Over the past thirteen years, I've observed my son as he has learned and reflected on how essential it is to tend the fire of faith behind the razor wire of a maximum-security prison. Jason once wrote this in a letter:

> *Mom, God is doing something powerful within me, and I'm very aware that I'm unworthy. Yet I often find myself speaking words that sustain the weary. I'm starting to experience something the prophet Isaiah wrote about in Isaiah 50: "The Master, GOD, has given me a well-taught tongue, so I know how to encourage tired people. He wakes me up in the morning, wakes me up, opens my ears to listen as one ready to take orders." And I know he is speaking to me personally about my own life too. Everything I find myself saying to others is a "sermon" to myself as well. I am nothing more than a fellow student, pilgrim, and spiritual traveler.*
>
> *One of the ways I'm experiencing more inner peace and spiritual freedom is through choosing to go to God in prayer early and often. First, before I try to strategize a plan or a path through the mazes of life, I ask him to make me wiser. Not because I have any innate ability to*

> *understand his plan, but because I am quicker than ever to turn to the only one who cares more than all of us and has the actual plan for our lives in hand. He desires conversation, fellowship, friendship, and communion.*

My heart leaped as I read my son's words. My prayers for him have not been answered in the way I hoped — with freedom outside of prison bars — but I have witnessed an extraordinary vibrancy in his faith that astonishes me. Jason has an intimacy with God that is richer, deeper, and more personal than at any time in the past. He has learned the secret of tending the fire by delighting in and meditating on, experiencing joy in, and lingering with and listening to God. The result of that relationship is purposeful living and following the voice of God as he has opportunities to use his leadership skills.

## The Turnaround Trip

It had been an intense season of ministry, and I knew I was behind on e-mail, social media, event planning, writing three endorsements for author-friends, and a writing deadline of my own. Why had I accepted the invitation to fly across the country from Tampa to Los Angeles for the television interview? I needed to be at home in my writing cave, working toward meeting my looming deadline.

But it was too late to cancel. The interview was being taped for a program that would later air in the English-speaking countries in the Pacific Rim. At the time I said yes to the invitation, I thought I could squeeze in time for the trip. I knew this opportunity would give me a chance to minister via television to people I might never be able to speak to in person. It seemed like a wise decision at the time, but I left for the airport reluctantly. To save time, I opted to get up at three thirty in the morning for an early flight to Los Angeles, and I planned to return to Tampa on the red-eye flight that would arrive at five thirty the following morning.

I had high energy for the five-and-a-half-hour outbound flight. Arriving in LA, I rented a car and drove for an hour to the studio in Simi Valley. The interview went well, and I sensed God's sweet blessing on the taping with the charming host from Australia. With the show wrapped up, I said my good-byes and began driving back to LAX. Ten minutes into the trip, I hit the rush-hour crawl. For the next two hours, I was in stop-and-go traffic, with aggressive drivers cutting me off. I made three wrong turns with the assistance of the GPS I paid extra to rent, and I wanted to throw it out the window every time I heard a relaxed female voice say, "Recalculating."

By the time I dropped off the car on rental row, rode the shuttle to the airport, waited in line to go through the TSA screening, and finally made it to my gate, I was frazzled and not looking forward to the all-night flight ahead of me. I opened my computer and turned to my Bible reading for the day. These words jumped off the page:

> "Are you tired? Worn out? Burned out on religion? Come to me. Get away with me and you'll recover your life. I'll show you how to take a real rest. Walk with me and work with me — watch how I do it. Learn the unforced rhythms of grace. I won't lay anything heavy or ill-fitting on you. Keep company with me and you'll learn to live freely and lightly."
>
> MATTHEW 11:28 – 30

I felt tears welling up in my eyes. There was a time in my early years of ministry when doing God's work was a joy and a privilege. When did it start feeling like so much work? When did I start viewing opportunities to share my faith with others as a burden instead of a privilege? I felt split between needing to maintain the appearance of a Christian on fire with passion for God and simultaneously feeling like an ash heap on the inside. I still believed in the truth of everything I spoke about, but the passion I once had for spending time alone with God was starting to feel more like an obligation.

I read the Scripture again: "Walk with me and work with me — watch how I do it. Learn the unforced rhythms of grace." I took a deep breath and allowed myself to consider what that would look like. I bowed my head and talked to God. *"Lord, I'm tired. I'm about as worn-out as I've ever been. Help me to get back the passion I once had and to relax in your unforced rhythms of grace."* I had come to the fire, and I sensed the Holy Spirit breathing fresh oxygen into my flagging passion.

It was finally time to board the plane. The flight attendant was friendly, a bright and shining light after a long day, and I enjoyed a brief exchange with her before settling into my window seat. Many hours later, we landed in Tampa, and I headed for home. That afternoon, this note arrived in my e-mail box.

*Dear Ms. Kent,*

*I had the pleasure of being your flight attendant during your flights to and from LAX yesterday. I was surprised to see you back on our evening flight and asked what you had done in the eleven hours we were in LA.*

*You told me you had done a TV interview. You radiated such grace and peace, I was compelled to Google you. I was*

*surprised to see the challenges you and your family have been through. I do wish you all the wonderful things God has provided and will continue to provide to your family. I hope to see you on another flight soon.*
*Sincerely,*
*Debi M.*

The note caught me totally by surprise. So soon after I had asked God to warm my cold heart and teach me how to experience "the unforced rhythms of grace," a flight attendant noticed a light on my face and took the time to contact me. It hadn't occurred to me that when we tend the fire, there is a reflection that touches those around us. God not only breathes new sparks into our own relationship with him; he also uses us to draw others to him at the same time. That knowledge — that we made a difference in someone else's life — increases our joy, and we burn all the brighter.

## More than a Checklist

As a driven perfectionist, I sometimes wish I could carry with me a checklist of everything I need to do each day to bring warmth to my relationship with Jesus. But the deeper I go with him, the more I understand that it's about far more than checking boxes on a list. Sure, a list of specific steps can help get me started, but nurturing my love for God is about a relationship, the rhythm of reading his Word, talking to him often, sometimes with my eyes wide open, and listening to his heart nudges as I actively seek to be a Jesus woman today.

It's about sensing his smile when I carry out a random act of kindness or when I stop midday to step outside and contemplate the exquisite beauty of the periwinkle-blue African lily in my yard — God's handiwork. It's about remembering a verse I memorized as a child, speaking it out loud, and being captivated with how relevant it is for a situation I just experienced. It's a heart attitude of seeing someone walk toward me or observing a name on caller ID and whispering, *"Give me your words for this person, Lord."* The more we walk and talk together, the more we love each other. And the less we communicate, the more distant I feel.

Do you, like me, sometimes struggle to make tending your relationship with God a top priority in your life? If so, you may find the following questions helpful. I use them to spot-check myself, especially when the busyness of life threatens to crowd out the important things in life.

- Is my spiritual fire being fed, or is it starving?
- Am I allowing the power of the Holy Spirit to breathe fresh faith and creativity into my dreams for the future?
- Am I pausing long enough to listen to God?
- Do I secretly feel like I'm wasting time when I block out time for Bible study and prayer?
- Are the noises around me drowning out God's whispers?

I'm still learning the process of tending the fire like David did:

O God, you are my God;
    I earnestly search for you.
My soul thirsts for you;
    my whole body longs for you
in this parched and weary land
    where there is no water.

I have seen you in your sanctuary
and gazed upon your power and glory.
Your unfailing love is better than life itself;
how I praise you!
I will praise you as long as I live,
lifting up my hands to you in prayer.
You satisfy me more than the richest feast.
I will praise you with songs of joy.
I lie awake thinking of you,
meditating on you through the night.
Because you are my helper,
I sing for joy in the shadow of your wings.
I cling to you;
your strong right hand holds me securely.

PSALM 63:1 – 8 NLT

David was a man who loved the Lord and longed to spend time with him, meditating on his Word, praising him in song, and lifting his hands in prayer. The more David meditated on God, the more his delight was fueled, and he loved him even more.

## Seasoned Wisdom

Gail MacDonald tells the story of attending a conference in a large arena where a retired missionary was about to speak. As the man ascended to the platform and moved in the direction of the lectern, Gail noticed the stooped shoulders and deeply set wrinkles of a person in his eighties — with the battle fatigue of one who had experienced years of spiritual warfare.

The challenge of his message was a simple statement that

became a marker moment in Gail's life: "Untended fires soon die and become just a pile of ashes." He went on: "The fire burns in the heart of the one who follows Christ. It is a flame that cannot go unmanaged, for if it is allowed to dwindle into ashes, the outer person is destined to a life of coldness."

Soon after Jason's application was turned down for the clemency hearing, I went through a period of dark cynicism. It had been so obvious that the letters we had meticulously collected weren't even read by the clemency aides before we were told the necessary waiver was denied. I found myself filled with distrust and skepticism. Subtly, the Enemy reminded me that God could have opened this door of opportunity for Jason's case to be evaluated, but he didn't. Instead, he allowed us to put two months of nonstop, heart-wrenching labor into collecting the letters of support. It felt unfair, and I doubted God's love. I pulled away from reading his Word on a daily basis and found myself spending much less time talking to him and voicing my praise and requests. I gave him the silent treatment, responding in forced bits and pieces, like a child who was offended.

God used the testimony of my son to warm my cooling heart. Jason wrote:

> Mom, I hate prison. But I will not waste prison. I choose to believe that God still has a purpose for me in spite of what I have done and the consequences I'm living with. The more I spend time in his Word, the more I understand the devastation I brought to you and Dad, to my wife, my stepdaughters, and to the family of my victim. I allowed my sin of self-reliance to grow in the weeks leading up to the murder as my fears and worries for my stepdaughters increased. I experienced a crisis of faith, and my actions

*have reaped death, devastation, grief, and the destruction of everything my life previously represented.*

*Now I am learning the power of going to God first when I'm faced with depression, relationship challenges, and the hopelessness that comes with a life sentence. I have been flat on my face before him, confessing my lack of faith and my failings, and there is a new kind of comfort and joy that comes over me as I sense his forgiveness and love. There are even days when I sense his delight in me as I seek to follow his leading on this compound. Joy, for me, is knowing as concretely as I know my name and my birthday that God is real and he loves me personally, and that I'm never alone and he can be trusted with my heart.*

Jason is learning the secret of tending the fire, and his example has challenged me to spend more time embracing and enjoying my love relationship with Jesus. When life is chaotic and disappointments crush my carefully made plans, my natural tendency is to work harder and longer, trying to escape the cacophony until exhaustion allows me to sleep.

After reading Jason's letter, I opened my Bible and read David's prayer:

God, make a fresh start in me,
    shape a Genesis week from the chaos of my life ...
Bring me back from gray exile,
    put a fresh wind in my sails! ...
Unbutton my lips, dear God;
    I'll let loose with your praise ...
I learned God-worship
    when my pride was shattered.

Heart-shattered lives ready for love
    don't for a moment escape God's notice.

PSALM 51:9 – 17

I found a quiet place and wept out my sorrow to God — prostrate before him, facedown on the floor — asking him to forgive me for distancing myself from him. As I felt the warmth of his embrace, I realized I had forgotten how good it felt to be close to him. I started singing, "I love you, Lord." I asked him to restore the joy of my salvation.

## Loving, Listening, and Responding

Thinking back to our reunion with Chelsea and Hannah reminds me that in every love relationship there are times of distance and times of closeness, and there are highs and lows. There are the moments of great joy and the challenges of walking together with difficulty, realizing there is the foundation of love even though communication is rocky. But the practices of tending the fire of my soul add fuel over time — meditating on his image, his words, his truth; experiencing the joy of his delight in me; listening to his voice; acting on his nudges.

As Gene and I were returning home from a ministry trip recently, we had a little time at the Indianapolis airport before our plane was ready for boarding. We revisited a restaurant where we'd had lunch the previous spring. Our waitress was a beautiful African-American woman who came up to our table with a big smile and said, "I remember the two of you! You were here a few months ago, and you gave me one of your books."

Then it came back to me. She was a young mother of four

children who was now a single parent after going through a challenging divorce. She said, "Your book helped me so much." We had a meaningful exchange with Sarah as we enjoyed our meal. When it was time to pay the bill, Gene pulled a twenty-dollar bill from his wallet to leave as a tip for our ten-dollar breakfast. He smiled at me and said, "God just told me to give Sarah a little encouragement today." I was warmed by the joy of observing the total delight on my husband's face as he responded to God's whisper.

Today I'm anticipating the adventure of taking enough time to listen to God's wisdom and heart, to see his smile on my life, to press into his embrace, and to be warmed by his presence. What about you? How will you tend the fire in your soul so that, rather than cooling to ashes, it crackles with life, roars back into life, and takes off in new directions? Such a well-tended wildfire could expand into new territory and spread farther than you can imagine.

## COME TO THE FIRE

1. Carol and Gene moved to Florida to be closer to their incarcerated son. What kind of sacrifices have you made as you've "tended" the relationships in your life? How about your relationship with God? In what specific ways have you been intentional about nurturing your faith?

2. Read Psalm 119:10 – 16. This passage identifies several ways we can tend the fire of our faith. Which way is the most difficult for you? Which, if any, do you feel curious about or drawn to? Why?

3. Luke 5:16 (NIV) reads, "Jesus often withdrew to lonely places and prayed." Do you have a favorite time and place to spend time alone with God? Do you have a favorite posture you use in prayer? Do you ever talk to God with your eyes wide open? What is your most common distraction when you spend time with him?

4. Jason quotes the prophet Isaiah to describe how God is teaching him "to listen as one ready to take orders" (Isaiah 50:4). How do you relate to Jason's experience? For example, what experiences have you had in which God put words in your mouth to encourage someone who needed hope, or directed you to take an action or make a sacrifice you might not otherwise have made? Record one of those experiences and share it with a friend.

## FIRE-BUILDING CHALLENGE

Marlae Gritter encourages women to plan ahead for "DAWG days" (Days Alone with God). What would you do if you had an entire day to concentrate on tending the fire of your faith? Make a list of the activities you would most want to do, Scripture you'd want to read, and a specific place you'd want to go. Check your calendar and pick a day to tend the fire of your faith. (Even if it can't be a whole day, try for a morning or an afternoon.)

CHAPTER 7

# Piercing
# the Darkness

We are told to let our light shine, and if it does, we won't
need to tell anybody it does. Lighthouses don't fire
cannons to call attention to their shining—they just shine.

D. L. Moody

It was a quick trip. I had flown to Virginia Beach to speak at a women's event, and one of my hostesses was a delightful woman named Cindee Riordan. Her optimistic attitude, energetic demeanor, and passion for ministry brightened the room. On our way back to the airport she spoke of her early roots, growing up on a small, square plot of land in rural Georgia. The town was settled by four families in the early 1800s.

I felt like I was stepping back in time as Cindee described the community of churches on Main Street and the juke joints on country dirt roads. I wondered what "juke joints" were and discovered they were informal establishments featuring music, dancing, drinking, and gambling. They were operated primarily by African-Americans in the southeastern United States and were often located at rural crossroads, catering to the workforce that emerged after the Emancipation Proclamation in 1863. The plantation workers and sharecroppers needed a place to relax and socialize, since they were barred from most white establishments. Cindee's portrayal of life in the Deep South was so powerful I asked if she would write out her description of the area she lived in and e-mail it to me later in the week. Her words were poignant:

*It smells of fresh fields of peanuts, corn, and cotton, yet has the lingering stench of bigotry. Graciousness abounds in homes, gardens, and shops despite being a district of poverty. The local folks are steeped in family traditions, kindness, and warmth, yet they are uncertain of how their traditional values and talents fit into a fast-paced global village. Pride dances with ignorance, and humility mixes with grace. Faith is found through the tears of sin.*

"Faith is found through the tears of sin"? That statement ignited my curiosity. My mind went back to our return trip to the airport, which was much too short. During that drive Cindee explained that, over the past few years, God had been at work to change the lives of both "perceived sinners" (prison inmates) and saints in this little town. "It's a place that has a story to tell," she said, "but it's not the one most Christian folks expect to hear." Why? Because it's the story of a church that was transformed by inmates, not the other way around.

I was captivated when I read Cindee's second e-mail, which explained the details of the story.

## The Beginning

It all started in the year 2000 when a popular retired sheriff named Troy Taylor went back to work for the sheriff's department as the administrator of the local jail. "We wanted to make some changes about how we rehabilitated the inmates," Troy said. "Many were young men with drug-related offenses, and we decided to launch a work detail with a county sentence rather than sending these young men into a state institution." As part of the work detail, the men began unloading food and repacking it for distribution through the food bank operated by the local Methodist church.

One afternoon, three inmates were working at the food bank with Troy's wife, Virginia, cleaning the empty community center to prepare it for the food distribution program. These young men offered to wash windows and floors — whatever was needed to get it ready. Virginia brought them lunch, and as they ate hamburgers together, she asked if they would tell her their stories of how they ended up in jail.

Henry described his parents' divorce, which ultimately led him to move in with his older brother. The problem was, his older brother was a drug user, and thus began Henry's addiction. The other young men's stories were much the same: Grant was a habitual drug user, and Jack had a series of bad relationships that led to his addiction.

Virginia was impressed with how thoughtful and helpful these young men were. As they talked during lunch, she thought, "These boys are no different from my own children." Virginia felt strongly that the young men needed to be part of a community, and her next step was to see about getting them into a church family where their faith could grow.

Virginia spoke with Troy and with Peter Fraser, the pastor of the Methodist church, and the three of them came up with a plan for a select group of inmates to start attending the eleven o'clock service on Sunday mornings. The inmates were called

"trustees" because they had made an effort to attend rehabilitation programs and earned privileges for good behavior. The
local sheriff signed off on the plan, and the trustees began
attending church with a member of the sheriff's department,
usually Troy Taylor.

Within a short time, the church added a Sunday school
class to help the trustees dig deeper into biblical truth. Many
were unchurched, and some were at the very beginning of their
faith journey. The teacher of the class was the county juvenile
judge, a man who had originally met many of these men in his
courtroom. This group bonded and soon became the largest
Sunday school class in the church.

Cindee explains:

Over the years, trustee families began to come to church
services so they could worship with their inmate loved ones.
The young men and their families would sit in the church
pews in their Sunday clothes as part of the congregation,
hearing words of mercy and grace. As Pastor Fraser said,
"I believe our call to the poor and to these inmates is not
always to go to them, but to bring them here and accept
them into the life of our church. It lets them be in ministry
to us and us to them." Eventually, the trustees and their
families made up close to one-third of our congregation.
Some of the regular opportunities for the trustees included
an annual Christmas luncheon with their families, a Super
Bowl pizza party, movie nights, and a recovery program with
weekly Sunday dinners.

In turn, the trustees served the church by helping out
with the food bank, Christmas decorating, and funerals.
Their contribution to the food bank program has continued
to be essential. Once a month, they pack over 600 bags

of groceries that help feed more than 300 families in a community of fewer than 7,500 people.

The editor of the local newspaper reported: "If you really want a workout, get in the middle of those trustees who are working in the food bank and try to keep up with them. They work hard and enjoy doing something good for others." Cindee said, "The program has been the catalyst for turning lives around."

By inviting these young men into their community, the church became a light that pierced the darkness. They did exactly what Jesus taught in the Sermon on the Mount:

> "You're here to be light, bringing out the God-colors in the world. God is not a secret to be kept. We're going public with this, as public as a city on a hill. If I make you light-bearers, you don't think I'm going to hide you under a bucket, do you? I'm putting you on a light stand. Now that I've put you there on a hilltop, on a light stand — shine! Keep open house; be generous with your lives. By opening up to others, you'll prompt people to open up with God, this generous Father in heaven."
>
> MATTHEW 5:14 – 16

A church that opens its doors to inmates and their families reflects what this passage is all about. But what happened in that church over the course of the next few months and years is nothing short of a miraculous *transformation* — in the form of an enduring wildfire faith that radically impacted lives and the entire landscape of a community.

## The Changing Heart of a Church

As the trustees became increasingly involved in the life of the church, there were rumblings of trouble — but not from the trustees. Cindee explains:

This church had a long-standing reputation of wealth and power in the community. Since we were in the Deep South, it was also a predominately white church before the trustees came to worship. There were families in our church that had sat in the same row, in the same pew, for generations. But when the trustees began attending, things were shaken up a bit.

There were church members who would not cross the aisle to shake hands with the African-American inmates, and they certainly didn't occupy the pews near them. Pastor Fraser saw this as a combination of them not wanting to change their long-standing prejudices and an unwillingness to face the fact that they might have more in common with the trustees than they wanted to acknowledge.

One elderly woman almost fell out of her pew when she saw one of the prisoners coming forward to take Communion. She called the pastor later that week to express her disbelief that this trustee felt "worthy" of Communion and made it clear that she certainly did not think he was. Pastor Fraser said, "There was a self-righteous, high-and-above-everyone-else attitude among some of the long-standing church members."

The trustees continued to attend services, and more and more of the African-American trustees attended with their families. This became an issue when an interracial couple started attending church, which meant there was now a black baby in the nursery. Some members of the congregation told Pastor Fraser that if he didn't turn the couple away, the church would lose folks. He refused. And sure enough, some members left. They said, "This just doesn't look like our church anymore."

But while some members walked away, many more stayed. There were still some who wouldn't reach across the aisle to shake hands with the trustees, but soon a group of church members formed a circle around the inmates in the pews and offered their authentic support and friendship. Troy Taylor, the man who had first brought the trustees to work at the food bank alongside his wife, Virginia, said, "I see a church now that is more accepting and far less racist." He continued. "Some have embraced this calling from God to minister to the inmates, while others in the congregation merely tolerated this mission. But now many of the wealthiest and most prominent members of the community are the ones who prepare Sunday night dinners for men in the recovery program and plan movie nights for the inmates. Community leaders teach the Sunday school class. By the grace of Christ, a community much like the one that followed Jesus has emerged, and together our church body has been transformed."

Talk about bringing out the God-colors in the world! What a beautiful image of a church that is truly "a city on a hill" whose light is visible to all. One of the church members said, "The diversity now found in this church has made a huge impact on all of us. The only people going to church now are those who love Jesus more than they love long-standing traditions and prejudices."

I love this story! What began as an effort to help inmates

became a fire that swept through a church, exposed hidden sins of prejudice, and then began to purge that prejudice. The result? God's glory now shines from that transformed church, reflecting the image of Christ to the rest of the world.

## What Does "Glory" Look Like?

In the Old Testament, God displayed his glory as an awe-inspiring expanse of bright light. It is often described as the *shekinah* glory of God — the visible manifestation of God among his people. This was the sign of his presence in both the tabernacle and in the temple (see Exodus 40:34).

When Moses said to God, "Now show me your glory" (Exodus 33:18 NIV), God responded not with a bright light but with a declaration: "[My name is] The LORD, the LORD, the compassionate and gracious God, slow to anger, abounding in love and faithfulness, maintaining love to thousands, and forgiving wickedness, rebellion and sin" (Exodus 34:6 – 7 NIV). In this case, God is declaring that his moral character demonstrates the glory of God for all to see.

When Jesus came to this earth as a babe in a Bethlehem manger, however, he emptied himself of the glory he shared with his Father before creation. When he came to earth, the breathtaking brilliance of the *shekinah* glory was hidden, except for the one isolated moment at Jesus' transfiguration.

So if the *shekinah* glory was hidden, how is it that the disciples testified, "We have seen his glory ... full of grace and truth" (John 1:14 NIV)? Because as great as the physical manifestation of *shekinah* light is, the glory of God's redeeming love is greater. Today, people who have been ignited by the spark of the gospel message don't physically display the *shekinah*, but they do reflect the light of God's glory when they love as Jesus loved and serve as Jesus served. God tells us to light our world with the light of his glory: "God said, 'Light up the darkness!' and our lives filled up with light as we saw and understood God in the face of Christ, all bright and beautiful" (2 Corinthians 4:6).

*The shekinah glory of God will pierce the darkness through you as you say yes to becoming his image bearer.* That is exactly what happened in a local church in a small town in South Georgia. And that is exactly what can happen when the flames of our wildfire faith light up our world.

From the perspective of the jail administrators in rural Georgia, there is no question that there were tremendous benefits when the inmates began attending church and having meaningful work in the community. Among other things, the number of men and women returning to jail as repeat offenders decreased, and in the trustee living quarters there were fewer fights and thefts. The transformation in the church was no less stunning.

Cindee describes what happened as God's light penetrated the hearts of the inmates and the church family:

For the trustees, involvement with the local church brought the joy of community and acceptance. Many experienced the transformational saving grace of Jesus Christ. They had the opportunity to worship with their families and a chance to begin the process of restoring their broken relationships. They encountered a faith that required them to step into the unknown and trust that God would be there. They found mercy when none was expected, and they discovered renewed hope when their hearts were more familiar with desperation. They not only received Communion, but they were invited to stand at the altar and serve the bread and wine to other church members. As a result, a church once known for its wealth and country club members became one of the most racially diverse churches in South Georgia.

The Bible says that heaven is a place of eternal glory. I never knew what that meant until I began to understand the meaning of the *shekinah* glory — God displaying his glory in a visual form as an awe-inspiring expanse of bright light. Since we will be with him in heaven, eternal glory will be the visible light of his presence among us all the time. And until we get there, we have the privilege of piercing the darkness on this earth by carrying his reflection everywhere we go. *A great privilege — and a huge responsibility!*

## The Power of Light

Soon after Jason was first arrested, I struggled with depression. On one particularly bad day, I closed all the blinds in our home, turned out every light visible to the front of the house, and wallowed in a sea of misery, with full knowledge that nothing could reverse the devastating circumstances of our lives. As my mind moved into heavy clouds of darkness, the Enemy fed me thoughts that led to the quicksand of despair:

"Your son will die by lethal injection if he is convicted of first-degree murder."

"Your ministry is a sham! Who would ever believe a biblical principle taught by you after you did such a disastrous job of parenting?"

"You will never come up with enough money to pay for a decent attorney."

"You dedicated your life to God when you were young and never turned away from him, but he still allowed this horrible thing to happen to your family. He must not love you."

"You are a complete failure as a Christian woman, a wife, and a mother. Look at all your friends. Their children are turning out just fine, but your child is a disgusting criminal."

"Your son's arrest negates every good thing you ever did for God in your lifetime. You are a total failure!"

In *When I Lay My Isaac Down*, I share a story about how my doorbell rang one afternoon when I was still in a quagmire of despondency. I peeked through a side window to see who was at the door because I was in no mood to talk to a reporter, or to anyone else for that matter. The vehicle in the driveway and the tissue-paper-covered vase in front of the stranger at the door were signals that no one would be asking me any questions, so I opened the door. With a much-too-enthusiastic voice for my dark day, the florist delivery guy said, "Hello, lady! Are you Carol Kent?" I nodded, and he continued. "Well, it's your lucky day!" he chirped.

In my dark emotional state, I muttered a quick, "Thank you." I wanted to yell, "Go make someone else's day lucky, mister!" But when you're depressed, you don't have the energy to produce a witty, quick retort, so I received the gift, walked it out to my kitchen, and placed it on the island in the center of the room. Tearing away the paper, I saw one dozen perfectly formed, long-stemmed yellow roses. At that exact moment, sunlight beamed in through the skylight, bouncing off the bouquet like an unexpected guest waiting for a welcoming smile. The sudden light lifted my spirits and made the gift even more special.

I opened the card. It was from two of my sisters.

*Dear Carol,*

*You once gave us some decorating advice. You told us that yellow flowers will brighten any room. We thought you needed a little yellow in your life right now.*

*Love,*
*Bonnie and Joy*

Tears welled up and spilled down my cheeks. I was so needy. I was in a deep, dark, emotional pit. I was hurting. Afraid for my son. Fearful for what the future held. Housebound by choice. Immobilized by shame. Guilty by association. And suddenly, through the loving gift of my sisters, a burst of light pierced through the veneer of my self-inflicted isolation and brought me a glimmer of Jesus-love — warm, accepting, hope filled, encouraging, and embracing. I was not alone. I was loved. The light of Jesus was shining through the yellow rose bouquet, through the loving card, through the tenderness of a tangible act of intentional kindness.

And the acts of kindness didn't stop there. One of my biggest surprises on the unexpected journey of having my only child incarcerated has been seeing how God continually uses people to pierce our lives with light in so many creative and tangible ways:

- Tommy, now in her eighties, sends Shoebox greeting cards with notes reminding me to keep some humor in my life.

- Doyle makes a generous annual donation to Jason's inmate account so he can bless the lives of incarcerated brothers who need personal hygiene items or postage stamps or would enjoy an occasional candy bar.

- My mother-in-law plans her trips to the prison around our ministry schedule so Jason has company when we are not able to get back in time for weekend visitation.

- Pam contacts Jason every fall and asks him to send her a Christmas card personalized from him to me. She picks out a uniquely special gift that is exquisitely wrapped and delivered to me with his card — empowering my son to do something special for his mom during the holidays.

- A church in Colorado sent a huge box of games, coloring books, and crayons for us to place in the prison visitation area so children have something enjoyable to do with their incarcerated fathers or brothers during their visits.

- Holly, who is married to one of the inmates, invited our family and the wife and son of another inmate to get together for a kayaking adventure last summer. Our shared challenges in learning to kayak provided the fodder for friendship and fun.

- Joannie sent a gift certificate for a meal out when our granddaughters came for their semester break from college. Her note simply read, "Praying for you! Make a memory!"

- Several of my author friends sent cartons of their books for us to distribute to the wives and moms of inmates who need encouragement and practical, biblical guidance.

- A meeting planner generously arranged for Gene and me to have an extra night in an oceanfront room on St. Simons Island following a weekend speaking engagement so we could relax and be refreshed after ministering to others.

All these acts of kindness have one thing in common — they spread the light of God's love in thoughtful and practical ways. Sometimes we think we need to do something big to make a difference, but I hope you see in all these examples that even a tiny spark can brighten a dark place with the glory of God. I recently heard from a woman named Alysia, who wrote, "Yesterday, I donated a pint of my blood to help an extended family member who needs my blood type. On the way to the American Red Cross, I dropped off a meal for a family with a mom who is struggling with the impact of treatment for pancreatic cancer. I can't save the whole world, but I can do something every day that helps at least one person who needs encouragement more than I do."

Have you experienced God's light penetrating your life during a dark time? Then you've experienced the power that light has to pierce the darkness. What have you done to carry the light of your faith into someone else's darkness? When God sets us on fire for him, he equips us with all we need to go from that first spark of faith through the most intense firestorms of life — and everywhere in between. The mystery and adventure of living out a wildfire faith is this: As the image bearers of Jesus Christ, we reflect his light everywhere we go. And the darker the circumstances, the more visible the light.

## COME TO THE FIRE

1. In what specific ways did the church in South Georgia reveal the brightness of God's Spirit? What were the

challenges? What were the risks? Have you ever been in a church that took a bold step in shining God's light into the surrounding community? Describe the results.

2. In the Old Testament, God displayed his glory as an awe-inspiring expanse of bright light. This *shekinah* glory of God referred to the indwelling of his presence — the visible glory of God among his people. Whom have you encountered who brightly reflects the image of Christ? (This can be someone you've read about or someone you know personally.) How has that person impacted your life?

3. Carol shared specific ways that the creativity of God's people pierced her family's life with brightness. What are some of the most loving ways someone has shown compassion to you? How did it impact you? How did it impact your faith and your relationship with God?

## FIRE-BUILDING CHALLENGE

Matthew 5:14 – 16 is inspiring:

"You're here to be light, bringing out the God-colors in the world. God is not a secret to be kept. We're going public with this, as public as a city on a hill. If I make you light-bearers, you don't think I'm going to hide you under a bucket, do you? I'm putting you on a light stand. Now that I've put you there on a hilltop, on a light stand — shine! Keep open house; be generous with your lives. By opening up to others, you'll prompt people to open up with God, this generous Father in heaven."

Make a list of specific ways you can "go public" with your faith. Pick one to accomplish this week — alone, with a friend, or with a group you're connected to. Use your social media platforms to explain what you did and to encourage others to find specific ways in which they, too, can shine the light and "bring out the God-colors in the world."

# CHAPTER 8

# The Refiner's Fire

Our Refiner will take what is impure and make it pure.
He will take what is dull and make it beautiful.
He'll take what is of potential value and reveal its
actual value. He will transform us into treasure.

**Kay Arthur, *As Silver Refined***

The prison visitation room was brightly lit by fluorescent ceiling lights. Gazing across several rows of tables where families sat with their incarcerated loved ones, I saw Deric, an inmate, handing out games to some of the guests. He had a smile on his face—the same smile that always greeted me warmly when I was there to visit Jason.

"How are you doing today, Mrs. Kent? It's good to see you." His friendly demeanor and big smile always surprised me because I knew that Deric, like my son, led a challenging life. Yet his face reflected an infectious joy. I found myself happy to be there as I watched him delight the son of an inmate by handing him a coloring book and a box of crayons.

I leaned across the table and whispered to Jason, "What's he in for?"

Jason gave me "the look," and I instantly understood that my question was inappropriate.

"Mom," he said, "on the inside we don't discuss the specifics of our crimes with each other. Deric is a committed Christian, and he's one of the strongest believers on the compound. We work out and pray together regularly. He lives out his faith every day, and I'm privileged to call him my friend."

"How long is his sentence?" I asked.

"Thirty years," Jason responded thoughtfully. "I'll die in prison if the current laws in the state of Florida remain what they are now, but eventually Deric will at least have an opportunity for parole." I felt that inevitable sense of hopelessness waft over me as I once again realized how *endless* my son's sentence is.

Several months went by, and I always enjoyed connecting with Deric when I came to visit my son. One weekend there was a different inmate in his place at the table where games are distributed.

"Where is Deric today?" I asked Jason.

"He's been moved to a prison closer to where his family lives," Jason told me.

I felt a deep sense of loss for my son, whose exercise and prayer buddy was suddenly gone, and for myself, because my connection with Deric had been a bright spot in every visit. I knew we might never again see this young man who had become our friend. One of the harsh realities of prison is that an inmate can be moved to any other prison in the state — without notice or opportunities to say good-bye to friends. For security reasons, the transfers usually take place at night.

A couple of months later, this letter from Deric arrived in our mailbox:

*Dear Mr. and Mrs. Kent,*

*I hope and pray all is well with you and with Jason. You may know I was moved to the Zephyrhills Correctional Institution, which is closer to where my mom lives. Being here will make it easier for my stepdad and mom to visit more often, and I'm hoping to get visits from other family members I haven't seen in more than twenty years.*

I was happy for Deric, knowing how much visits mean to inmates. Having a caring family close enough to come to the prison often provides great encouragement. A harsh reality for those who are behind prison walls is that, statistically speaking, after five years of incarceration, most inmates with life sentences or long sentences no longer have family members continue to visit them. My heart was comforted to know that Deric would be able to see his family members more often. I read on.

*Zephyrhills is a medical prison facility and it's now my job to care for dying, elderly, and disabled inmates who will more than likely finish their lives here. I bathe them, brush their teeth, change their diapers, and empty their catheter bags. I help them get in and out of their beds, wheelchairs, and gurneys.*

A wave of nausea swept over me as I realized the difficult labor Deric was now required to do in exchange for the transfer to a prison closer to his family. His letter continued.

*Every day while I feed them and shave them I tell them about Jesus, or sometimes I just let them talk and get things off their minds. I've had the privilege of comforting several who were crying and freaking out.*

*Recently, I read Scripture to an eighty-one-year-old inmate who had prostate cancer. I really liked him. Five hours later he died. This is a sad, hard, dark place, but I know God wants me to be here, and I want to be here.*

*I can tell God has changed me a lot in the two months since my transfer. I just want to be like Jesus. I want to do God's work and not be afraid to ruffle feathers or to take verbal abuse because of my obedience to God. I want to be respectful and not a people pleaser ... I work about seventy-two hours a week right now, so I need prayers for strength, energy, and a good attitude.*

*Tell Jason I miss him and hope to see him again — if not here on earth, then in heaven where we will meet up and hang out together. Ask him to greet all the guys at Hardee for me and ask them to pray for me too.*

*May God bless you and keep you bringing men and women to him.*

*Your friend and brother in Christ,*
*Deric*

I was in a puddle of tears as I finished Deric's letter. By the renewing power of the Holy Spirit, he is a transformed person. God took a man who had done something wrong enough to earn a thirty-year sentence and is walking with him through the refining fire. Now, after more than twenty years in prison, his punishment has not changed, but the clear image of Christ in him is reflected every day to the dying inmates he serves.

## What Is the Refiner's Fire?

Refining gold and other precious metals by fire is a process that has been used since ancient times and is still used today. The refiner places the gold in a crucible — a container used for melting metals — and tends the flame by adding more fuel and fanning the flames with air from the bellows. As the gold melts in the intense heat (typically around 1,832 degrees Fahrenheit), impurities called dross rise to the surface. When the refiner carefully skims away the murky dross, he can gaze into the molten metal and see a clearer but still somewhat distorted reflection of himself. He lets the fire cool, then once again builds it up and repeats the process with an even hotter fire. This releases another layer of impurities that rises to the surface and is skimmed off. The process is repeated until, finally, the refiner gazes into the liquid gold and sees nothing but his crystal-clear reflection.

Biblical writers often draw on the image of the refining process to illustrate how God purifies us:

> The crucible for silver and the furnace for gold, but the Lord tests the heart.
>
> Proverbs 17:3 NIV

> [God] knows the way that I take; when he has tested me, I will come forth as gold.
>
> Job 23:10 NIV

> "See, I have refined you, though not as silver; I have tested you in the furnace of affliction."
>
> Isaiah 48:10 NIV

How does God test the heart? How does he reveal our hidden motives? How does he expose our wrong thinking? He uses our circumstances to "turn up the heat," refining us into the crystal-clear image of Christ.

Even though I understand that this is one of the ways God works, I can't help but wonder why God couldn't come up with an easier way for us to become reflections of his image. Yes, as God's Word tells us, he reshapes us into the image of his Son in many ways. For instance, his Holy Spirit dwells within us and fills us with the fruit of the Spirit; his Word, when we meditate on it, reshapes our thinking; and fellowship with other believers brings growth and spiritual development, just to name a few. But the simple truth is that sin has so infiltrated our character, our heart, and our mind, that sometimes nothing short of God's refining fire can purge those deeply tangled knots of sin that trip us up and take us captive time and again. The apostle Paul describes our plight well:

> For I do not do the good I want to do, but the evil I do not want to do — this I keep on doing. Now if I do what I do not want to do, it is no longer I who do it, but it is sin living in me that does it.
>
> So I find this law at work: Although I want to do good, evil is right there with me. For in my inner being I delight in God's law; but I see another law at work in me, waging war against the law of my mind and making me a prisoner of the law of sin at work within me. What a wretched man I am! Who will rescue me from this body that is subject to death? Thanks be to God, who delivers me through Jesus Christ our Lord!
>
> ROMANS 7:19 – 25 NIV

Of course, the sacrifice of Jesus on the cross saves us from the eternal consequences of our sin, and once we are in heaven we will sin no more. But while we live on earth, we, like Paul, contend with our sin nature. If we are to more clearly reflect God's light on this dark earth, then we must submit to the Refiner's fire.

In suffering, the moral impurities of our character rise to the surface, allowing us to see them as God purges them from our lives. We should never confuse this refining process for punishment for our wrongdoing. All of us have sinned. All of us fall short of the glory of God. The Refiner's fire is not punitive; it is life-giving, though painfully so. The heat of such hard times actually improves us, drawing us closer to the heart of God and enhancing the way we reflect his character. Deric, in caring for the sick and dying, reflects the love and compassion of God to those who desperately need to see it.

So how can we experience unquenchable faith in a furnace-like experience? How exactly does the proven genuineness of our faith "result in praise, glory and honor when Jesus Christ is revealed" (1 Peter 1:7 NIV)? The longer I live, the more I realize this result is much more of a *journey* than it is a *destination*. Like Deric, like the men with leprosy in the next section, and like my friend Katie, whose story you are about to read, there are no instant shortcuts from the Refiner's fire to the state of purity when we finally and fully reflect the image of Jesus. There is only the journey and the confidence that the longer we endure, with our hearts set on reflecting him, the more Christlike we become.

## The Ultimate Outcast

The lepers of biblical times were outcasts. Forced out of their communities, they were considered unclean, and anyone who came into contact with a person with leprosy was defiled. Talk about a group of people who knew what it was like to live in the middle of a fiery trial! Matthew's gospel tells the story of one such person.

> When Jesus came down from the mountainside, large crowds followed him. A man with leprosy came and knelt before him and said, "Lord, if you are willing, you can make me clean."
>
> Jesus reached out his hand and touched the man. "I am willing," he said. "Be clean!" Immediately he was cleansed of his leprosy. Then Jesus said to him, "See that you don't tell anyone. But go, show yourself to the priest and offer the gift Moses commanded, as a testimony to them."
>
> MATTHEW 8:1 – 4 NIV

If you take a close look at the leper in this story, you will see he demonstrated an astonishing confidence in Jesus when he said, "You can make me clean." Everyone knew leprosy was incurable. Even so, I imagine Jesus' merciful response shocked not only the bystanders who witnessed it but also the leper himself. Jesus reached out his hand and *touched* the man, saying, "I am willing." Did Jesus need to touch him to heal him? No. So why did he? Why would he touch someone who was considered literally untouchable? Allow me to share a brief story that sheds light on what I believe to be the reason.

Several years ago, I was invited to speak at a retreat sponsored by the Evangelical Community Church of Hong Kong. That's where I met Ruth Winslow, a missionary to China who works as a health care professional and vocational counselor, primarily in rural villages with people who have been cured of leprosy. Drugs are now available to cure this dreadful disease, but any damage done before the medication is administered is usually not reversible. Though they are medically cured, the former lepers are "marked" by their scars and considered detestable. In China, many are still forced to live as outcasts in government-designated areas.

I was immediately attracted to Ruth's compassion for these rejects of society who know what it's like to live in the crucible of suffering. I asked her to tell me more about her work. Her face lit up as she shared one of her experiences.

One day she was washing the ulcerated feet of a man in the remote village where she works. His feet had been disfigured by leprosy over many years. Having his feet touched was highly unusual. As his eyes met hers, he softly whispered, "Thank you."

Without hesitation, Ruth responded, "Thank Jesus."

A quizzical look crossed his face as he looked her in the eyes again and spoke, "*You* are Jesus."

Who has been Jesus for you in a time of suffering? When we are in the Refiner's fire, sometimes we need a loving touch. God often uses his people to wait with us, walk with us, pray over us, weep with us, hurt with us, and forgive us. And as hard as it gets, as long as it takes, these stick-like-glue representatives of Christ continue to get personally, tangibly involved in our journey. Jesus provided that example when he touched the man with leprosy instead of just healing him with a spoken word. What a joy when one of God's people reaches out to us to help us in our time of need! Katie was one of those people for me. Then she found herself in the crucible.

## Katie's Crucible

I met Katie when we were both working on a writing project. Her buoyant spirit, energetic demeanor, and unique creativity fueled my passion to work on ministry projects that would outlast my life. She was there for me when Jason was arrested and when we walked through the dramatic, heart-crushing two and a half years and seven postponements of his trial. She always had a listening ear and a word of encouragement. Nearly a year after Jason's arrest, Katie told me of her own crisis. Here is her story:

My name is Katie, and I'm married to a sex offender. Without my knowledge, my husband inappropriately touched our teenage daughter over a period of time. There was never a time when I suspected anything amiss between Craig and Lindsey. They were loving and playful and never appeared to be distant or awkward around each other.

During her teen years, I was concerned about some ongoing health issues Lindsey was having. I took her from doctor to doctor and was continually told she had a bad virus and would eventually kick it. Then I was told she had a weakened immune system. I even took her to a Christian counselor, who said there were no unusual circumstances that contributed to her health issues. But I knew there had to be something at the root of her illnesses.

One day I received a call from our local children's advocacy center requesting that I come and talk to them about an issue with Lindsey. I panicked, and my mind went in multiple directions. Upon arriving, I was ushered into a private room with a counselor from the center.

"Your daughter, Lindsey, has accused her father of sexual assault. We have questioned her at length and believe she is telling the truth."

I was so shocked I couldn't believe what I was hearing. "What if it's a false accusation?" I blurted out. "She's lied to me before. I can't believe her father would do such a thing!"

"I know this is hard for you, but we videotaped her allegations," the counselor said. "Would you like to watch the video?"

"No," I replied, sinking further into a black cloud. If this were true, I couldn't bear the thought of seeing her agonize in front of strangers, telling a camera what her father had done to her. Then a police detective came into the room. I looked to him for a way to understand what was happening. It felt like I was in someone else's bad dream.

"Couldn't she be lying about this? I've heard about false memory syndrome and about false allegations to get attention. Could this be what it is?" At that moment, I was desperate for a different explanation.

"I've been involved in a lot of these cases," the detective replied, "and I have a good sense of when someone is being truthful. This is not a small thing; it's not like her taking a cookie out of the cookie jar and lying about it."

The weight of his statement hit me hard. What had my daughter actually lied to me about that was like this? Nothing. As much as I could not comprehend my husband doing what she accused him of, I knew she was telling the truth.

I thought we were a typical family that loved Jesus and loved each other. We raised our family on biblical principles. We served at our church and led Bible studies. My husband was a church deacon, and we were a part of the worship team. I felt my world crumbling around me. I was in such a state of disbelief that it startled me to hear the detective speak again.

"Your husband is being confronted by the police right now. You can call him if you like and ask him about it; he knows what he did."

Another stabbing wound to my heart. A fierce anger welled up inside of me. My mother-heart was breaking, and inside my head I was screaming.

I made the call to Craig and angrily said, "What have you done to Lindsey?" All I could think about was what a terrible thing this was for Lindsey to suffer. What a despicable, wicked thing!

"The police are here right now," he whispered into the phone. "Do you believe all those things they are saying about me?" I could hear the panic and fear in his voice.

"You know what you did. I can't believe you would do that to our daughter!"

The detectives had hoped he would confess on the spot, but he didn't. I have little recollection of the rest of our short conversation. At that point my thoughts were only for Lindsey.

The advocacy center counselor asked if I wanted to see Lindsey, and I immediately said yes.

Lindsey came into the room, and I reached out and hugged her, my heart filled with grief. "Is it true?" I gently asked. She nodded yes and pressed into my shoulder as I whispered in her ear, "I am so sorry."

For Katie, this was the beginning of a long journey of discovering how abuse affects the victim, the secondary victims (her youngest daughter, Susan, and herself), and the perpetrator (her husband, Craig). Her story continues:

Lindsey and I drove home in an unsettled quiet. Craig was not allowed to talk to or see either of the girls, nor could he return home for any reason. After the initial shock, he found mercy with his Christian boss and his wife. They invited him to stay in their home during the first week. At his request, I took him some clothing and toiletries. It was embarrassing and humiliating for me to go to his boss's home. They were more than gracious, but in my shock I just moved through the motions that would get me in and out of their house as soon as possible. My anger flared as I went into the guest room for my first encounter with Craig. I spoke in a hateful voice: "It's going to be a long time before you see the girls."

This horrific day continued as I sat down later that afternoon with my thirteen-year-old daughter, Susan, to tell her what happened. She adored her father. I spoke slowly and calmly, but inside my stomach was wrenching and my heart was pounding with anxiety. I didn't know how I would tell her. "God, please help me," I prayed.

We sat together on my bed. "Honey, your daddy won't be home for a while. He did something bad, and the police won't let him come home."

Susan's eyes welled up with tears. "What did he do?"

It was time for the words I had been dreading to speak. "He touched your sister inappropriately."

With disbelief in her eyes, she responded with anguish, "On purpose?"

"Yes," I said.

Susan grabbed me around the waist, buried her head in my chest, and sobbed. Her sobs were filled with pain, and I couldn't help but join with her, overcome with that same pain myself. Susan had just lost her father—it was as if he had died in a plane crash. She had seen him that morning and now would not see him again for a long time. The abrupt change to her life was staggering.

For Lindsey, it was the release of a secret she had kept far too long, one that was eating her alive and affecting every aspect of her life. It was also the opening of a Pandora's box of emotions so large it spewed anger and bitterness everywhere.

Perhaps you've been in a situation where your world was shattered and there were layers of disappointment, pain, hurt, disillusionment, anger, or even depression. This can happen through a sudden change in health, an accident, a job loss, a financial crisis, a struggle with infertility, a child's wrong choices — any of a multitude of difficult circumstances. If you were momentarily stopped in your tracks, how did you transition to a place of hope, or are you still struggling to find your way?

## The Fire Got Hotter

The next step for Katie and her family was a meeting with the Department of Human Services (DHS) and then with Family Court. Four months later, Craig pleaded guilty before a judge and was sentenced to ninety days of work release and five years of probation. His sentence also mandated participation in a sex offender treatment program, which included weekly group therapy, frequent polygraphs, and court fines. Katie explained:

> The first few months were horrific—between Craig and me, and for me at home coping with the girls' emotions and needs while working full-time. I often asked myself, "How could he cross that line? How could his values be so different from mine? How could he be so selfish?"
>
> If Craig had not confessed to our pastor, making himself accountable to him and to the leadership of our church, if he had not earnestly repented of his sin, and if he had stolen Lindsey's virginity along with her innocence, I don't know if I would have stayed with him. My husband had turned my world upside down. I was angry and hurt, and I had lost all

trust in him—as a father, a husband, and a brother in Christ. But this one thing I know—God is faithful. Because of that truth, I determined to cling to God and to do what was right in his eyes.

Craig and I started finding answers together. I often went to the Psalms and prayed, "Restore to me the joy of your salvation and grant me a willing spirit, to sustain me." As time passed, I finally became willing to begin the process of forgiveness.

Soon after his arrest, Craig started seeing a Christian counselor in addition to attending the required group therapy sessions he had begun even before his conviction. A few weeks later, I joined him. While our Christian counselor helped us find the road to recovery, God also used a fourteen-week couples' Bible study group to profoundly change our lives. As we worked through the marriage study and immersed ourselves in Scripture, we found our trust slowly rebuilding.

As part of his court-mandated restrictions, Craig couldn't attend church or be anywhere near places where children might congregate. Knowing our life in Christ was the very foundation on which we needed to rebuild, we asked God to reveal a way for us to meet our spiritual needs as a couple after we completed the Bible study. God answered that prayer by leading us to a chapel in a local hospital. We met there for four and a half years on Sunday mornings for ongoing Bible study, discussion, and prayer. We learned much about each other and about our God. Craig learned how to cherish me, and slowly I grew to respect him. That chapel became a sanctuary for us.

After nearly two years, Lindsey, by God's grace and through the influence of our new youth pastor, found it in her heart to forgive her father. This sensitive, Holy

Spirit–empowered pastor had been severely abused as a child and knew both the internal conflict of a desire for vengeance and the benefits of releasing anger and choosing to embrace forgiveness. Lindsey cried for two hours after talking with him and wrestled with God for about two more months. Soon after, Lindsey was ready to face her father.

Their first meeting, referred to as an apology session in the sex offender program, took place in a counselor's office. Craig had been prepped for how to behave (let Lindsey initiate any physical contact; don't touch her otherwise; let her lead), and Lindsey previously met with the counselor to confirm her desire for this meeting. As Craig walked into the room, he was seeing Lindsey for the first time in more than two years. The first moments of that meeting were powerful. Neither the counselor nor Craig was prepared for the words they would hear.

"Dr. Smith," Lindsey said straightforwardly, "I have something to say to my father, and I don't want you to interrupt me.

"Dad, I love you, and I forgive you. I've met the man I want to marry, and I want you to walk me down the aisle."

After regaining his composure, Craig, a broken man, read his apology letter to Lindsey.

Just five months earlier, Lindsey had referred to Craig as "a sperm donor" and said she had no feelings for him. But on this day, after intense counseling, prayer, tears, and emotional healing, Lindsey's unselfish act of forgiveness brought about reconciliation with her earthly father.

Following this meeting, Katie and her family slowly journeyed through the remaining two and a half years of Craig's sentence. And just as Jesus reached out and touched the leper,

Craig, Katie, and the girls were touched by the continued support of a powerful prayer team at their church. Katie supervised meetings for Craig with Lindsey and Susan in public places, and finally, Craig successfully completed the sex offender treatment program and his five-year probation.

Katie told me, "As time passed, God moved our family into his complete redemption. I not only have a caring and compassionate husband; I have two beautiful daughters who, for a season, struggled and pulled away from me and from each other. But God has restored our love and made it stronger than before. Today, as a family, we delight in using our resources to build God's kingdom."

Today, both Lindsey and Susan are married, and Craig and Katie are grandparents to Lindsey's daughter. Lindsey, as well as Susan and her husband, work in the family business, and they all attend church together. A sweet blessing for their family is that their senior pastor is the same youth pastor who ministered to Lindsey more than fourteen years ago.

The story of Katie's family stands as a remarkable story of healing and redemption and the hard work of enduring the process with the end in mind. I would be remiss, however, if I left the impression that sexual abusers should always be brought back into the home or that a loving Christian response requires such liberty to the offender. Craig's recovery took years of earnest submission to God's discipline, legal requirements, mandated and voluntary counseling, and true repentance. Some offenders are never able to make that journey successfully, or the damage they have done to another is never, here on earth, able to heal to the point that reunion is wise and healthy. But even in those cases, God can bring repentance and forgiveness, along with continued protection for the abused.

An offender can be forgiven but still required to pay the earthly consequences of his or her acts. What truly matters are the eternal restoration of hearts before the Lord and the gift of the Refiner's fire, though painful, that purifies the hearts of entire families. The story of Katie's family shows us that their faithful endurance paid off.

## We Are His Treasure

When our lives are in a crucible, the Refiner never leaves us unattended — he never steps away from the fire. It's hard for me to understand this excruciating process, but I am beginning to realize that the finished product he longs for demands this painful evolution. As he bends over the flames and as the dross of our lives rises to the surface, he skims off the ugliness of our wrong choices through the process of confession and forgiveness.

Pastor John Piper wrote, "There is no painless path to heaven. Why? Because Jesus said, 'Blessed are the pure in heart, for they shall see God.' And it is no more possible to become pure painlessly than it is to be burned painlessly. Purity comes through the refining fire."

I wish this process could be shorter for Deric, the inmate working over seventy hours a week in the medical unit of a Florida prison. I wish my friend Katie did not have to go through the personal devastation and public humiliation of her husband's conviction as a sex offender. And I continue to long for an eventual end-of-sentence date for my son. But the hidden treasure in each of these experiences is the discovery of the image of God himself reflected in the precious metal that has been purified.

Are you willing to submit to the Refiner's fire for the goal of reflecting God more clearly? When the heat is turned up, it's hard to remember that God's intent is not to destroy us but to purify us. Our response to the process is crucial.

Will you cooperate in removing impurities, or will you resist or rebel? I admit I'm not good at achieving this every day, but I am striving for Job's mind-set: "When he has tested me, I will come forth as gold" (Job 23:10 NIV). Endure, strive, and keep your life focused on reflecting the love and character of God to the world.

# A Postscript

You may have read this chapter and thought, "Thank the Lord I am *not* in the Refiner's fire!" If that's the case, I'm happy for you. But I also want to challenge you to be intentional about touching the hand of the person going through an unspeakable ordeal, especially if that person is a sinner whose behavior has repelled you in the past.

Before reading the next chapter, will you pause long enough to think of someone in your sphere of influence who is in the middle of the Refiner's fire — either because of what God allowed to take place or because of his or her own wrong choice — and will you intentionally touch that person by doing whatever God prompts your heart to do?

## COME TO THE FIRE

1. Scripture uses the refining process to illustrate how God purifies us until he sees his own image reflected in us (Job 23:10; 1 Peter 1:7). Whom have you observed

in the crucible of suffering who is coming through it in ways that reflect the image of Christ? How would you describe the changes this person experienced?

2. God often uses his people to wait with us, walk with us, pray for us, weep with us, hurt with us, and forgive us. Who has been that kind of a comfort to you during a difficult time? In what specific ways did this individual help you make it through your ordeal?

3. Carol quotes John Piper: "There is no painless path to heaven. Why? Because Jesus said, 'Blessed are the pure in heart, for they shall see God.' And it is no more possible to become pure painlessly than it is to be burned painlessly. Purity comes through the refining fire." Even though most of us agree with that statement, we still see some Christians who seem to have pain-free lives. How do you respond to this tough question: Is God always fair?

## FAITH-BUILDING CHALLENGE

What do you think modern-day social lepers look like? List some ways you or a team in your church could minister love in Jesus' name to a specific group or individual. Then prayerfully form a plan of action to do something tangible to help like Ruth Winslow did when she washed the feet of the man with leprosy.

CHAPTER 9

# When Flame
# Meets Flame

Jesus, God's lens through whom his love is
uniquely focused, translates our splintered lives into
something from which he can ignite warmth and life . . .
God sends trials not because we are strong enough
to struggle through them but to help us grow strong . . .
and the life that springs up around the edges
of endeavor redeems what may seem like tragedy.

**Luci Shaw,** *Horizons*

The call came late at night. My sister Paula was on the other
end of the line — and she was sobbing. It was hard to piece
together the story because she could hardly get the words out:
"Michael shot up the house. I left and called the police, but he's
still inside firing shots through the walls. I'm so afraid." With
the assurance that the police had arrived, I tried to console my
sister, who was terrified.

Later, the local newspaper revealed more of the details:

> A judge Wednesday ordered that a Florida man charged
> with attempted murder of a police officer be jailed and
> then held under house arrest until trial.

Michael Johnson, 37, will wear an electronic moni-
toring bracelet in his home. The bracelet will allow law
enforcement officials to keep track of Johnson, who allegedly shot at his wife and two sheriff's deputies during a
domestic dispute at the home on Wednesday, March 4 ...

Judge Anthony J. Markham said that according to
a report, Johnson "shot up everything in the house that
reminded him of his wife." One bullet apparently went
right over a sheriff's head and hit a squad car ...

The Johnsons had been seeing a counselor, and their
marital problems "came to a head." On the night of the
domestic dispute, Paula Johnson left the home and called
the sheriff. A standoff began at 7:45 p.m., when Johnson
allegedly fired shots from a scope-equipped rifle at his wife
and sheriff's deputies ...

Johnson held sheriff's deputies at bay and kept his
neighbors away from their homes almost three hours ...
[before he] surrendered to about forty Special Operations
officers [and] was taken to a mental health center.*

What had gone wrong? My own sister, a victim of domestic
violence? But it was true. I later learned more about the details
that led up to this devastating night. Paula was twenty years old
when she married Michael. She said, "On the first day of our
honeymoon, I thought, 'Have I just made the biggest mistake
of my life?' In spite of abuse and unfaithfulness, we remained
married for seventeen years. I'd been taught that divorce is
a sin. My parents were in the ministry, and I didn't want to
damage their reputation. Besides that, I loved my husband

---

* This is a factual portrayal of my sister's story, but some names have been
changed to protect the privacy of people involved.

and didn't want to be single. After we had a child, I thought I shouldn't break up the family because of our son."

Paula told me that one of the hardest parts of the marriage was not knowing if her husband would be in a happy mood or be mean and violent when he came home. She said, "I learned to deal with both personalities, but not knowing which person was going to walk through the door was hard. Michael and I had some great times, full of fun and laughter, but on the flip side, there were extremely frightening times." Then she gave birth to Tony. When their new baby was only three weeks old, Paula discovered her husband had just approached one of her best friends, seeking an affair.

She thought, "How could I have been so delusional to think having a baby would solve our marital issues, let alone stop his infidelity?" Today, Paula would tell you this was an early lesson in how God can provide a blessing even in the midst of a bad situation. She describes early motherhood: "Our son was born perfect. He usually slept at night, was almost always happy, ate well, and learned to speak early. Tony was a pleasure to parent, but my marriage issues were getting more intense."

When Tony was nine years old, Paula separated from her husband. Michael constantly begged her to come back, and finally she agreed to give it a try. By this time Paula had been meeting with a counselor, and Michael agreed to join her at one of the appointments. But during the session he became so enraged that the psychologist asked him to leave. After trying to make the marriage work for several more weeks, Paula realized she needed to get out while she was still alive. She put a deposit down on a condo but needed to wait to leave the home she shared with Michael until her application for residency was approved.

Five days later, her husband called her workplace and demanded that she come home immediately. She later learned he had gone through her purse and found receipts that indicated she was leaving him again. Their home was in a remote country area on five fenced acres. Leaving her car outside the gate to the driveway, she walked up to the house and entered through the side door of the attached garage. She immediately noticed the garage door window was shattered and there was glass everywhere.

Michael owned a large gun collection and a lot of ammunition that was usually stored in the attic, but it was in full view as she walked into the house. As she entered the kitchen, he started to come toward her as he yelled, "Get out! Get out now before I kill you!" Before Paula was able to leave the room, Michael threw his full drink and her briefcase into the living room wall so hard they both punctured the drywall.

As Paula fled to her car, she heard three gunshots, but she wasn't hit. Trembling, she dialed 911 as she drove out to the road. Speaking to the dispatcher, she said, "My husband is in the house with guns. He fired three shots, and I don't know if they were aimed at me or at himself." The dispatcher told her to drive to the nearest corner and wait for the sheriff.

Before the night was over, forty officers — representing the local sheriff's department, the K-9 unit, and the SWAT team — and two police helicopters were at my sister's home. Michael barricaded himself in the house and staged a standoff by turning off all indoor lights and turning on all outdoor lights as he randomly shot through the walls of his own home. He yelled, "The only way I'm coming out of this house is in a body bag!" Three hours later, he responded to a telephone call from the police officers and agreed to be taken away for psychological evaluation. The next morning he was released. The report indicated he was not suicidal or psychotic, just an obsessed lover. The police allowed him to return home, saying he had only shot up his own personal property.

My sister filed for a lifetime restraining order. Michael was arrested and spent two weeks in jail before being placed under house arrest for six months, but he did not go to prison. Paula's marriage ended in a painful divorce. Over a period of seventeen years, she experienced escalating personal challenges that grew from small marriage problems into abuse, infidelity, and eventually terrorizing fear. Her relationship with Michael was out of control.

## Two Kinds of Wildfires

While it's true on one hand that wildfires in nature can be frightening, destructive, and deadly, when wildfire is used as a metaphor for faith, it takes on a whole new meaning. It represents a faith that harnesses that same kind of raw, unstoppable power — but this time for eternal good. Instead of destroying, it purifies. Instead of taking life, it gives life. Instead of traumatizing, it transforms.

On the other hand, I purposefully used the metaphor of a firestorm in chapter 2 to describe a horrendous trial. Why? Because some trials are so raw, so seemingly unstoppable, that fire seems the perfect image to convey how their effects can traumatize, destroy, and leave scars on lives.

When I picture what wildfire faith looks like, I think of the apostle Paul. However, the faith of his early life was more icy cold and calculating than wildfire hot. As a devout Pharisee with a stellar family tree, Paul described himself as "a Hebrew of Hebrews" (Philippians 3:5 NIV). His ancestors could be traced all the way back to the ancient Israelite tribe of Benjamin. Although it's hard to imagine in our time and culture, Paul was highly respected because of his legalism. He had also gained a distinguished reputation among his constituents for his commitment to persecuting Christians. Paul would later refer to his legalistic, "faultless" life — when he was still known by his birth name, Saul — as self-righteousness.

Then, as quickly as a lightning strike ignites a wildfire, his life was changed one day on a Damascus road. He was blinded by a brilliant light and heard a voice from heaven:

> He fell to the ground and heard a voice say to him, "Saul, Saul, why do you persecute me?"
>
> "Who are you, Lord?" Saul asked.
>
> "I am Jesus, whom you are persecuting," he replied.
>
> ACTS 9:4 – 5 NIV

Talk about drama, confrontation, and special effects! This story is complex and exciting. Saul had a hit list of people he was intent on persecuting — in God's name — and the Lord basically turned Saul's world upside down by telling him he was, in fact, persecuting the God he sought to defend. This is the kind of story that goes way beyond what any Hollywood producer could come up with.

After his conversion, Saul was renamed Paul, and as we read about the rest of his life, we see what God can do with one person who says yes to wildfire faith. His transformation included horrific suffering, dangerous missionary journeys, controversial public speaking events, terrifying threats, and multiple incarcerations — all of which were mixed with great joy, miraculous answers to prayer, intimate friendships and ministry relationships, and a lot of letter writing. He is credited with penning thirteen books in the New Testament, and many of those manuscripts were completed while he was in prison, without benefit of computer or Google searches!

In light of everything we know about Paul's unwavering faith, I have often wondered why God did not take away what Paul described as his "thorn in the flesh." Surely he must have been one of God's favorites. Why would God allow him to continue suffering? Paul wrote:

> I was given the gift of a handicap to keep me in constant touch with my limitations. Satan's angel did his best to get me down; what he in fact did was push me to my knees. No danger then of walking around high and mighty! At first I didn't think of it as a gift, and begged God to remove it. Three times I did that, and then he told me,
>
> > My grace is enough; it's all you need.
> > My strength comes into its own in your weakness.
>
> Once I heard that, I was glad to let it happen. I quit focusing on the handicap and began appreciating the gift. It was a case of Christ's strength moving in on my weakness. Now I take limitations in stride, and with good cheer, these limitations that cut me down to size — abuse, accidents, opposition, bad breaks. I just let Christ take over! And so the weaker I get, the stronger I become.
>
> 2 CORINTHIANS 12:7 – 10

This extraordinary testimony reveals one of the secrets of wildfire faith. Our faith grows stronger, more unquenchable, more powerful, and more visible in the middle of our most intense limitations. Nineteenth-century British evangelist George Müller acknowledged this paradoxical trust in God that is intensified by the heat of suffering when he wrote, "The only way to learn strong faith is to endure great trials."

May I be brutally honest? I hate this truth. I want a different path — for my son, for my husband, for me, and for my sister too — but I've already learned the power of this principle as I've watched my sister's story unfold.

## Unstoppable Blazes

After Paula's divorce from Michael, she eventually fell in love again and married a pilot. John worked for a major airline, and they relocated to Texas. John treated Tony like his own son, and the two had mutual love and respect for each other. However, ten years into Paula and John's marriage, two things happened that destroyed the stability of Paula's new life: toxic mold and infidelity. John and Paula learned that their house had extremely high levels of poisonous mold, and they had to move out of their lovely home immediately. Then Paula learned that John was cheating on her — and it wasn't just an affair; he was actually living with another woman in his main layover city. Her second marriage ended in a second divorce.

The mold caused medical problems for Tony that were severe and long lasting. He initially needed six-hour blood infusions once a week for six weeks. Although he was able to begin college the next year at Texas Tech in Lubbock, Texas, he continued to struggle with his health and lost over one hundred pounds. He loved university studies, but he needed to come home to get healthy. After two years, he eventually transferred to Texas State University in San Marcos, Texas. One morning Tony called his mom, and through tears he said, "I can't get up. My head feels like it's going to explode. I have no idea how I wound up on the couch." We later learned that Tony had just experienced his first grand mal seizure.

The neurologist's assessment was sobering. "This will be a complete lifestyle change." Paula felt like she was in someone else's nightmare as she heard the doctor address her twenty-five-year-old son. "You can no longer live alone. You can't drive, ride a bike, or swim." Both Paula and her son were numb with the realization of the permanent changes that would be taking place in his life. Tony began having such severe and uncontrollable seizures that none of his friends wanted to take on the responsibility of living with him. During the next year, my nephew was hospitalized twenty times. A plan was worked out that meant Paula would stay with Tony at his apartment most of the time, and his best friend, Jared, would stay overnight when she couldn't be there.

Because he was taking massive doses of antiseizure and antianxiety medications, Tony had very poor balance. After a major fall that splintered a rib and aggravated his lung tissue, he had severe chest pains, followed by two thoracic surgeries. Finally, Paula was able to take him back to his apartment. A few weeks later, he said, "Mom, I'm twenty-seven years old, and I need my privacy. I don't want to live with my mommy." Her grown son chuckled and said, "I love you, but please go home."

Truthfully, Paula was ready to go home. Tony seemed to be on the mend, and he was getting stronger. She left, and they communicated often. A few weeks later, he phoned and said, "It's time for you to stop worrying about me, Mom. I love you.

Good-bye." He didn't call her the next day, and she didn't call him either. She called the following day, but he didn't answer. Then Paula sent him a text message. No reply. On the third day there was still no response, so she called Jared and asked him to check on Tony. He immediately headed to the apartment and called Paula soon after arriving with the shocking news that he had found Tony, and he wasn't breathing. What he didn't tell Paula was that Tony was decomposing. She later found out he had likely passed away three and a half days earlier from complications exacerbated by his seizure disorder.

Paula said, "He was gone. My son, my only child, was gone. My brilliant child, who was four classes away from graduating magna cum laude, was gone. Why?"

I agonized with my sister over the loss of her precious son — not the quick death of someone in an automobile accident, but the long, debilitating death of watching her straight-A, university-student child deteriorate mentally from the dulling of the antiseizure drugs and physically from the ongoing falls that caused broken bones and the never-ending hospitalizations. It was a cruel death.

Two of our sisters, Jennie and Bonnie, immediately flew to Texas to support Paula emotionally and to help with the multiple decisions that had to be made. Their presence during this agonizing experience was a God-kiss to our heartbroken sister. I admit I continue to ask God why he allowed my sister to go through two excruciatingly painful divorces followed by the death of her only child. Why does a God of love allow things like this to happen? Is there a redemptive reason behind this severe sorrow? Why is God often hidden and silent during the worst moments of crises in our lives?

At this stage of my life I'm discovering I prefer honest questions more than superficial answers. I believe my questions are OK with God. He is sovereign, and I am not — and he and I both know there will be questions I have that will only be answered in heaven. I'm not OK with that, but that's what I have to work with right now. And he loves me anyway.

The day after the memorial service for Tony was Paula's birthday. As it turns out, the anniversary of my son's conviction for first-degree murder is two days before my birthday. Both Paula and I would like to permanently quit celebrating our birthdays — and not just because we're getting older. The devastating memories surrounding those dates are a constant reminder of our pain.

Paula spent her birthday emptying her son's apartment with a small army of Tony's friends who showed up to help. It didn't take long to divvy up his few earthly possessions and send what remained to the Salvation Army. Paula said, "And that marked the end of a very special phase of my life. How does one say good-bye to a child? I mean really say good-bye, forever good-bye, it's-all-over good-bye? Tony's friends went home. Life went back to normal for everyone — except me."

## Surviving a Firestorm

At this point, my sister had survived the firestorm devastation of losing her son, but her recovery was just beginning. She was overcome with grief and pain. When I have found myself in such times, I often take comfort in these words from the prophet Isaiah:

> To care for the needs of all who mourn in Zion,
> give them bouquets of roses instead of ashes,
> Messages of joy instead of news of doom,
> a praising heart instead of a languid spirit.

Rename them "Oaks of Righteousness"
   planted by GOD to display his glory.

ISAIAH 61:3

It's a beautiful image, isn't it? But what does it look like in real life? How does God use his people to show his love in that way?

On the day she returned home to Houston after cleaning out Tony's apartment, Paula found a birthday card from me waiting in her mailbox. I included some cash and a little note, suggesting that after everything she had just gone through, I'd love to treat her to a manicure and a pedicure. Money was tight for Paula, but that day, with birthday money in hand, she stopped by a coffee shop on her way to the nail salon. Paula placed her order with the woman working alone at the counter: "I'd like a grande caffè mocha."

The woman rang up her total, and as Paula was getting ready to pay, the barista said, "No charge for you today." My sister was stunned and asked why the drink was free. The response, in a kind Asian accent was, "Because that is what computer say." The woman turned the screen toward Paula and read the exact words: *No charge for you today*. Paula smiled, and her imagination went wild. Tony was a "supernerd" with computer technology. With a touch of humor, she envisioned her son, now in heaven with superpowers, doing something sweet for her as a way of saying, "Good-bye, Mom. I love you."

Paula then walked next door to the nail salon. After getting settled in one of the spa chairs for a pedicure, something unexpected happened. Tears began flowing down her cheeks, and the woman seated next to her noticed. Paula said quietly,

"Please excuse me. I just lost my son." Suddenly, this lovely woman took Paula's hand in hers and began praying out loud for her. There was silence in the salon as this woman demonstrated Christian compassion in action.

When it was time for Paula to leave, she went to the counter to pay, and the cashier said, "No charge for you today." Paula could hardly believe her ears. The woman continued. "You have been through enough."

Sometimes God turns our ashes into beauty through the kindness of total strangers. Loss is hard, and Paula went through many more tearful days. But that day God demonstrated his love for her in tangible ways that gave her unanticipated encouragement and brought the warmth of hope and joy to her heart.

## A Future We Cannot See

As much as I hate to admit it, the apostle Paul was right. Our faith *does* grow stronger in the middle of our most intense trials and limitations. I want a different, easier path. I'm still grieved by the depth of depression and sadness my sister has endured, but I'm also rejoicing that she has come through to a place of new life, vibrant faith, and a different kind of joy.

In fact, one of my son's favorite visitors at the prison is my sister. He calls her "Auntie Foo Foo" because she brings fun, drama, delight, and encouragement into the visitation room when she enters. Paula and Jason have known great sorrow, but they have also experienced great joy — the anticipation of a better future in a place where Tony is now free from pain and in a place where there will be no more tears.

Today I was at the prison visiting my son — again. Nothing

has happened to change his life sentence. But I'm choosing to start a new kind of wildfire — one that spreads hope, not because of what we see today, but one that focuses on a future we can't see. Yet. The apostle Paul reminds us:

> So we're not giving up. How could we! Even though on the outside it often looks like things are falling apart on us, on the inside, where God is making new life, not a day goes by without his unfolding grace. These hard times are small potatoes compared to the coming good times, the lavish celebration prepared for us. There's far more here than meets the eye. The things we see now are here today, gone tomorrow. But the things we can't see now will last forever.
>
> 2 CORINTHIANS 4:16 – 18

I marvel at my sister's resilient spirit and her determination to live for a future she cannot see. Multiple firestorms of horrendous destruction have torn through her life, yet each time they've collided with her wildfire faith, her faith has won the battle. I believe that her decision to live with her eyes on her future with God has been her secret weapon for spiritual victory.

My friend Tanya is facing down her own collision of fires — wildfire faith versus firestorm. Like Paula, Tanya's life has been spent at the fire wall.

I met Tanya four years ago at a Speak Up Conference. She was there to work on honing her speaking skills, and I was in the audience with an evaluation form. My job was to give her a helpful critique, but I soon found myself overcome with emotion and unable to evaluate in my usual way. Tanya's story is best told in her own words:

I had never known a father's love. Those things we all think of—daddy/daughter dances, strong arms to rescue us, protection, safety, unconditional love, and affirmation— these had been the furthest things from my personal experience. From the time I was two until I was fourteen, each man in my life, including my biological father, my stepfathers, and my grandfather, had taken their turn as thieves to steal from me sacred things that were never meant for them. Sexual, emotional, and physical abuse characterized my relationship with anyone I had ever called "Father." Control, manipulation, and fear summarized my experiences with those I called "Daddy."

When I came to Christ, my way of loving the Father was simply to allow him to love me. Like an overly tired infant who has nothing to give, it was a good day when I could rest enough and trust enough to simply allow him to offer me comfort rather than flailing about in life, consumed by my own misery. Each time I was willing to become vulnerable enough to spend time in his presence, seek his face, and hear his voice, he was faithful, gentle, and patient, leading me ever so slowly into those deeper places of intimacy with him.

After years of relationship, trust came more easily. As he healed my heart, making every broken place whole, the scales of fear, mistrust, and suspicion fell from my eyes, helping me to see my Father clearly. I came to experience what I longed for most—a tender, loving relationship with my Father.

Tanya married, and she and her husband, Luke, had two children, Brooke and Tyler, who are now teenagers. About to complete a degree in biblical counseling, she was speaking and writing from a heart she describes as "burning steady" when the unthinkable happened. Thirteen-year-old Brooke had not been feeling well, and after undergoing multiple tests, she was diagnosed with T-cell lymphoblastic lymphoma. As I write, it's been nearly eight months since the diagnosis, and Tanya is still in the middle of the firestorm.

Over the last several months, I have experienced heartache deeper than I have ever known. The initial days of crises were filled with anguish—the shock of the discovery of the tumor, the days in ICU, the surgeries for biopsy and port placement, the beginning of chemo. It all happened so fast. Luke and I never left her alone at the hospital. I remember breaking away while he was there to run downstairs for coffee—taking a few moments to call and give updates, sitting outside in the little hospital courtyard, sobbing deeply while people walked by, ate their lunches, and carried on with life.

For four months, I wrestled with my faith. The very God I encouraged others to run to was suddenly someone I felt I could not run to. The very Scripture I offered others in times of disappointment held no comfort for me. I cycled through the emotions of anger, confusion, fear, and resentment. How could God, who loves us, allow this to happen? Why didn't he protect us from this awful, dreadful thing?

It felt ridiculous to pray to him for healing or comfort in light of knowing that he knew this was coming and allowed it anyway. The encouragement offered by others—"He is with you; he never leaves or forsakes you"—was no comfort either. A Father who allows pain and suffering, standing by and watching it happen, was all too reminiscent of a childhood filled with abuse.

So for the first four months, I refused to talk to him. I

couldn't. I had nothing to say. My world had been shattered. The peace and comfort I was desperate for were beyond what any human could offer me. I can't even say I fought the battle in my own strength. I mostly just hurt, cried, feared, and mourned our losses as they came. I just survived.

All the while, I felt guilty. I knew I was not responding the way a "good" Christian should respond. I was shocked and disappointed in my own lack of faith, my inability to "fight the good fight." I felt like a hypocrite. A minister of the Word, one who stood on platforms and encouraged others to run boldly to the throne of grace—no matter what—and I couldn't do it myself.

It took a while, but eventually my desperate need for God overcame my anger. Truth offered from the closest of friends helped me to realize that my feelings of betrayal stemmed from false expectations. I searched the Scriptures to find what I had believed was there—and came up short. I couldn't find any Scriptures that said nothing bad will ever happen to me or to those I love. I couldn't find any Bible verse assuring me that my life on this earth would be pain free. What I did find, however, were numerous Scriptures assuring me that *when* trouble came, God would be with me. *When* difficult situations arose, his grace would be sufficient. That instead of fear or worry I could allow the peace and comfort of the Holy Spirit to fill me, while I kept holding fast to the truth that perfect love casts out all fear.

Brooke now has two intensive months left in her treatment. She will have massive chemo injections followed by steroids that devastate her emotionally—bringing tears, depression, and anxiety. She will have long procedure days, with spinal taps two weeks in a row, followed by the medicine that has made her the sickest of any of the chemo meds — often taking her a week of vomiting to recover. During this time, she will be isolated from her friends and her church.

Tanya expressed her feelings with these words:

The calendar tells me we will officially complete the weekly treatment schedule in just under two months, which will be nine months since we began this journey. I'm trying to find that place of "only two more months to go" in my brain and in my heart, but I'm struggling. Instead of relief, I feel sad and exhausted. Looking at what is ahead, I feel I have nothing left—that Brooke has nothing left—not enough energy or strength to make it. Nothing hurts like watching your kid hurt—nothing!

I asked Tanya to describe the biggest firestorm she'd ever faced in her Christian life. "A year ago," she said, "I would have told you it was the death of my mother, the loss of a longed-for relationship that never was, or the sexual abuse I experienced as a child. But now I can say, without a doubt, that it has been Brooke's diagnosis and her battle with cancer." She went on:

When I contemplate the arduous journey we have traveled and are traveling still, I can't help but feel overwhelmingly thankful for the privilege and ability to stand next to Brooke and fight. We have encountered too many parents from whom that privilege has been stolen, too many children who have lost their lives in the midst of the battle. And I am thankful there is a treatment that combats this dreadful, life-stealing disease. The bottom line is—I *know* the Lord will be faithful to continue to be my strength and hers, but this journey is unthinkably hard.

Within the first few months of Brooke's treatment, Tanya and I talked on the phone, and I ached for her as she sobbed out her pain. But she did not stop in her pain. She pushed through, wrestling with God and pursuing his presence in the midst of her suffering.

## Reflections on Suffering

Tanya's story has no easy answers. My son, Jason, is still on a journey that includes more questions than answers. Paula's story is still one of ongoing healing. What about your story? Is your wildfire faith dukin' it out with a firestorm? You may be asking many of the same questions Paula, Tanya, and I have asked:

Does God answer prayer? *Yes, but sometimes differently than we expect.*

Does God protect us from pain? *Not always.*

Does going through an intense firestorm mean we will be freed from more storms in the future? *Absolutely not.*

If we are faithful to God, will life be pain free? *You already know the answer to that question.*

But what is your answer to this question: In the battle between your wildfire faith and your firestorm, which fire wins?

Author Robert Farrar Capon writes, "He comes to us in the brokenness of our health, in the shipwreck of our family lives, in the loss of all possible peace of mind, even in the very thick of our sins. He saves us *in* our disasters, not *from* them … He meets us all in our endless and inescapable losing." As hope-filled as those words are amid the firestorms of our lives, it is Jesus who gives us the greatest comfort of all. He said, "In this godless world you will continue to experience difficulties. But take heart! I've conquered the world" (John 16:33).

Jesus Christ has conquered the world. He has conquered sin and death as well. In the next chapter, we'll explore the ultimate strategy for enduring the fires of this world while living out our wildfire faith.

## COME TO THE FIRE

1. Wildfires in nature can be frightening, destructive, and deadly. When *wildfire* is used as a metaphor for faith, however, it represents a faith that harnesses that same kind of unstoppable power, but for eternal good. Instead of destroying, it purifies. Instead of taking life, it gives life. Have you experienced a time when an unwanted personal firestorm accelerated the growth of your faith? What happened, and what did you learn?

2. God used women in the coffee shop and in the nail salon to show his love and compassion for Carol's sister Paula during one of the lowest points in her life. When you look back on a time when your heart was hurting, what specific thing did someone do to give you hope or help you to experience God's care for you?

3. This chapter describes what happens when the fire of suffering meets the God of the flame. Robert Farrar Capon wrote, "He saves us *in* our disasters, not *from* them." In what ways would you say God has protected, surprised, and encouraged you when you were experiencing a difficult time? How did he save you *in* your hardship?

## FAITH-BUILDING CHALLENGE

Use a Bible reference guide (such as a concordance or an online reference tool) to help you make a list of ten names or attributes of God. Write a brief sentence after each one that describes how you hope the God of the flame will meet you at your point of greatest need. Here are two examples to get you started:

*God is my shield:* He provides protection from the Enemy.
*God is my El-Shaddai:* He is my all-sufficient supporter.

# CHAPTER 10

# Unquenchable Faith

I need a God who is with us always, everywhere, in the
deepest depths as well as the highest heights. It is when
things go wrong, when good things do not happen, when
our prayers seem to have been lost, that God is most
present. We do not need the sheltering wings when things
go smoothly. We are closest to God in the darkness.

Madeleine L'Engle, *Two-Part Invention*

It had been an unusual year. Amid a schedule filled with speaking at conferences and retreats, Gene and I started receiving invitations to speak at prisons. Whenever we were in a city where we could take an extra day and minister to inmates, we said yes. However, as familiar as I was with prisons, I wasn't prepared for what happened on the day we passed through security and entered the chapel at Okeechobee Correctional Institution in South Florida.

There was Matthew Ben Rodriguez in the front row. He had been one of my son's best friends at Hardee Correctional Institution, where Jason is currently incarcerated. Matt and Jason are about the same age. Matt is clean-cut, well-spoken, intelligent, and passionate about Jesus. But he pulled a trigger one day in a botched robbery attempt, and a woman died. According to Florida law, Matt — like Jason — will die in prison.

Matt had been relocated to this prison a year earlier, and I missed seeing him and his mom and sister visiting when we visited Jason. A few years earlier, Tammy Wilson, the daughter of the woman Matt shot and killed, had attended an event where I spoke. Tammy later looked up my son on the Internet and discovered he was in the same prison where Matt was serving a life sentence without possibility of parole. She e-mailed me the following week, told me her story, and asked if Jason would be willing to contact Matt and introduce him to Christ. If you read my book *Between a Rock and a Grace Place*, you already know we then discovered that Matt was already a strong believer. But through this connection, Tammy gave me her address to share with Matt, and multiple letters passed back and forth between Matt — the murderer — and Tammy and her sister and brother, the children of Matt's victim.

I knew I was standing on holy ground as I witnessed the miracle of forgiveness extended by Tammy and her family to Matt in the middle of their unthinkable loss. They approached Matt with tender humility, generosity, and compassion. Matt expressed gut-wrenching remorse for his actions and sorrow for the pain he'd caused. The willingness of Tammy's family to accept Matt's request for forgiveness deeply touched the core of my own faith.

I hugged Matt, having no idea if regulations allowed that, but my mother-heart could not resist embracing my son's dear friend. I had grown to love that boy. "How are you, Matt? We miss seeing you at Hardee. Is your family doing OK?"

I took my seat up front along the wall of the brightly lit chapel, with a full view of the inmates who now filled every available seat. The inmate worship team began to sing about the blood of Jesus that washes away every sin. They belted out, "Blessed be your name on the road marked with suffering." The guitarist, trumpeter, keyboardist, and drummer were gifted, and the inmates lifted the roof off the chapel with their voices of praise to Almighty God. I tried to sing, but my eyes were filling with tears, and I found myself in the middle of a room full of faith more intense than I had ever experienced before. The faces of the men reflected a spiritual fire that was contagious. Unstoppable. Knowing that many of those who gathered that day were "lifers," I wondered:

What kind of faith refuses to die?

What makes faith unquenchable?

How does a Christian — like Tammy Wilson — tap into a relationship with God that is so red-hot that forgiving the unthinkable becomes possible?

How do men who made devastating choices in their youth and received life sentences keep on living in such a difficult place when there is no hope of being paroled for good behavior?

Why does their faith seem stronger than my faith?

Later that same week, I spoke at another prison, this time in Central Florida. Following the message, the inmates lined up to greet us. One took my hand and said, "I was in the same prison as Jason last year, and he shared his faith with me. At that time I was a member of a cult, and I had totally rejected Christianity. Please tell your son that I follow Jesus now, and I want to thank him for his bold witness. Even though Jason didn't know it, God used his words to open my heart to truth."

OK, I admit it. This mama wiped away some tears. I was profoundly overcome with the collision of old dreams I'd had for my son that I had to let die to make way for the stunning eternal purposes God was now fulfilling through Jason in prison. This isn't the way I wanted my son to spend his life. Turning gray-headed behind bars was not on my wish list for my only child. Would I have wanted him to serve in missions? Well, maybe — but not in full-time ministry inside a state penitentiary! Yet, as I witnessed God using Jason for his kingdom purposes, how could I not give thanks and marvel at such a miracle?

When I returned home, I picked up my Bible and read this passage:

> Do you see what we've got? An unshakable kingdom! And do you see how thankful we must be? Not only thankful, but brimming with worship, deeply reverent before God. For God is not an indifferent bystander. He's actively cleaning house, torching all that needs to burn, and he won't quit until it's all cleansed. God himself is Fire!
>
> HEBREWS 12:28 – 29

This is the secret of wildfire faith — *that God himself is Fire!* Fire reveals our true character. It purifies. It refines. Fire spreads. It reshapes. It dispels darkness and brings warmth. It gathers a crowd of witnesses. Fire cauterizes as it seals wounds from the past. I now realized what I had seen on the faces of the inmates in the prison chapel — the *shekinah* glory of God reflected on the faces of redeemed men who have confessed their sins and are growing in their faith. Their faith ignited hope in the hearts of their fellow inmates. Their faith was so pure and rich and honest that I felt humbled and honored to be in their presence. Their sins had been forgiven, and their spirits set free.

The same is true for you and for me. Our sins are forgiven, and we, too, can take up residence in God's "unshakable kingdom."

## Exploring a Great Mystery

I have heard inspiring stories from Christian men and women who have experienced profound miracles. Some have been pronounced cancer-free after initially receiving a terminal diagnosis; others have undergone a slow, agonizing death. Some with addictions have entered Christian rehabilitation centers and permanently turned their backs on substance abuse. Others continue in a self-destructive lifestyle, causing great hardship for their families. I recently received this letter from a woman with a drug-addicted son:

> I am a divorced mother of two children, and I receive no support from my ex-husband. My teenage son has been in and out of jail repeatedly due to his addiction to cocaine. I wanted to save him from a wasted life and sold my home in order to pay for his long-term treatment in a Christian environment. Now, six months after being declared healthy, he is back on the streets. My faith is wavering, and I am struggling financially. Why did God allow this to happen?

So how is it possible to sustain a wildfire faith when God appears to answer the prayers of some people but withholds his favor from others? Is there a secret answer to this question that hasn't been revealed? What did Oswald Chambers mean when he wrote, "Faith is deliberate confidence in the character of God whose ways you may not understand at the time"?

I went back to Hebrews looking for an answer. A verse I memorized as a child stood out to me: "Now faith is being sure of what we hope for and certain of what we do not see" (Hebrews 11:1 NIV, 1984 ed.). As a child, I believed this verse meant that even when I don't see a positive resolution for my problem, I can rest in the knowledge that he is God and I am not. In other words, things will turn out in the end because I have faith. That seemed easy to believe — until my son was arrested for murder.

Reading further in Hebrews, I came across those heroes of faith who experienced great spiritual victories. Daniel was saved from the mouths of lions. Shadrach, Meshach, and Abednego were kept from harm in the intense flames of the fiery furnace. Elijah escaped Queen Jezebel's henchmen. Gideon was powerful in battle, and God used Elisha to bring a widow's son back to life. All these stories and many more remind me of the kind of mountain-moving faith we have access to as Christians. These dramatic accounts inspire and motivate me to have great faith in an all-powerful God of love and mercy.

But then comes a troubling passage:

> There were those who, under torture, refused to give in and go free, preferring something better: resurrection. Others braved abuse and whips, and, yes, chains and dungeons. We have stories of those who were stoned, sawed in two, murdered in cold blood; stories of vagrants wandering the earth in animal skins, homeless, friendless, powerless — the world didn't deserve them! — making their way as best they could on the cruel edges of the world.
>
> HEBREWS 11:35 – 38

I like to skip right over those verses because I don't have a good explanation for why God provided in a miraculous way for the Hall of Famers in the first part of this chapter but then allowed others to experience torture, abuse, homelessness, and rejection. Does this mean there is no connection between having a wildfire faith and an easier life?

I see a clue to the secret of unquenchable faith in this passage. Every one of the people the Bible talks about was looking forward to something better. They were looking ahead to their true home:

> Each one of these people of faith died not yet having in hand what was promised, but still believing. How did they do it? They saw it way off in the distance, waved their greeting, and accepted the fact that they were transients in this world. People who live this way make it plain that they are looking for their true home. If they were homesick for the old country, they could have gone back any time they wanted. But they were after a far better country than that — *heaven* country. You can see why God is so proud of them, and has a City waiting for them.
>
> HEBREWS 11:13 – 16

Although they died without tangibly holding what was promised, they had an eternal perspective, and as a result they were able to look at life as a place they were passing through, not as a destination.

Will you do this? Will you endure the pain of this broken world, knowing you are just passing through, that you are on the road to a better country — *heaven* country? Even though you do not yet have in hand the paradise promised to you, do you see it way off in the distance? Will you accept the fact that you are a transient in this world and that your real home, your permanent home, is just ahead, perfectly prepared for you? This is the kind of wildfire faith that will endure *anything*!

As you're about to see, these were the choices Agnes had to make.

## A Heart on Fire

I first learned of Agnes from my friend Gerry Gardner, whom I'd met at a women's conference. Gerry was there to speak about her extraordinary mission, and my heart was immediately drawn to her passion. She has personally ministered to women who have experienced the chaos of suffering, but she has also discovered that wildfires change the landscape of our lives, and that sometimes on this side of heaven — and sometimes not — we will discover that God's purposes and plans are far beyond our limited vision. She shared:

> I remember the day clearly and the grief they all wore — the women of Rwanda. It was early April, and I stood looking at the row of nineteen wooden coffins and the purple crosses carefully sewn to the white cloths draped over them. I drew in a deep breath as I was told how each coffin represented the remains of at least twenty individuals who had been killed in 1994 when genocide destroyed this tiny country. Well planned by Hutu extremists in power at that time, more than 800,000 people were killed by clubs, guns, and machetes in just 100 days. Men, women, and children — no Tutsis were to be spared as the extremist members of the

majority people group called Hutus cooperated with the orders to inflict genocide. And now here I was in Rwanda in 2007, praying as the grieving families continued to bury their dead.

As I stood there on that very warm spring day, the pictures I had viewed the day before at the Kigali Genocide Memorial Centre continued to play in my mind, gruesome beyond belief as they depicted the slaughter and the malicious disfigurement that happened at the hands of the perpetrators. Man's inhumanity to man. I struggled with my own response—my lack of tears. I was too numb to comprehend how this horrific genocide happened in Rwanda, a country that was ostensibly 85 percent Christian in 1994.

I had been asked by the director of the mission to say a few words at the commemoration. *How does one really prepare for such a moment?* Then I thought back to the day before when I had arrived precisely at the time when a widow was asking ministry leaders to come with her to view the remains of her family—remains that had been in a mass grave for thirteen years and had been found just that week. I stood with this widow as she looked at what was left of her mother and sister. Amid the decay, her mother's dress was still recognizable, as was the bracelet on her sister's arm. God have mercy! On this commemoration day, she would finally have peace as her family members were given a proper burial.

Standing in front of the attentive crowd, I began with the only words my soul would allow me to speak: "I humbly ask for your forgiveness for my own part in the genocide. I was forty years old when it began. I remember reading a newspaper and seeing a black-and-white photograph of slaughtered bodies on the far right page of the paper." With tears in my eyes and a choking voice, I admitted, "I simply turned the page. My prayers were needed, and I did not pray. My voice was needed, and I did not speak. My participation was needed, and I did nothing about your pain."

It mattered to me that they heard this day a validation of the bigger act of indifference that took place globally. It mattered to me that I acknowledged the shame of my own heart, standing there and seeing the dire consequences of a world that chose not to listen to the Rwandan cries for help. It was hard to receive the words of thanks that came from many of those present who heard my words. Being thanked for a confession of the soul seemed to be a painful act of mercy from ones who had suffered so much.

The spark that ignited Gerry's call to missions was unexpected, personal, poignant, and deep. She was simply a volunteer who picked up a guest speaker for her church — but God started a fire in her heart that day.

Watching the burials that day, I remembered the car ride that had changed my life just two years before. A young Anglican priest from Rwanda was in the United States to speak on behalf of a reconciliation ministry, and I had been asked to pick him up and transport him to our church. Father Philbert Kalisa told me that he was born of Rwandan parents in exile in Burundi, his family having fled from Rwanda back in 1959 when conflict was escalating for the Tutsis. He had been in seminary in England at the time of the genocide in 1994 but went back to Rwanda in 1995 to see what had happened in his country. That's when the Lord spoke to him, asking him to return to Rwanda and begin a healing and reconciliation ministry. No one in Rwanda wanted to hear that kind of message so soon after the atrocities. There was so much grief, so much hatred, so much devastation, but

Father Philbert and his wife began a ministry they called REACH (Reconciliation, Evangelism, and Christian Healing), which brings together genocide survivors and perpetrators.

During the forty-five-minute car ride from the airport, he spoke, and I listened. That day, the fire of God's Spirit branded my heart with a connection to the people of Rwanda. As we pulled into the parking lot at the church, we both knew something significant had happened, though neither of us could find words. My tears spoke volumes. We sat for a few minutes in silence, sensing God's presence. As I opened the car door, I knew God was calling me to minister to the women of Rwanda.*

The day I met Gerry, I asked if she would send me the story of one of the women she had met — someone who had captured her heart through the fiery strength of her relationship with Christ. A few days later, Gerry sent an e-mail, and I was captivated by the heart-stopping story of Agnes, a woman with wildfire faith.

*I met Agnes on my first trip to Rwanda as we sat in a church with a dirt floor, windows open to the hills. I had listened to the testimony she gave that day in front of the other genocide survivors. She stood stoically, facing the crowd. She wore folds of colorful material wrapped around her tall figure and a white cloth draped over her shoulder. She spoke in her native tongue, Kinyarwanda, barely taking a breath for over forty-five minutes. The interpreter whispered in my ear, making sure I could hear but not disturbing the hush over the room as Agnes spoke. She told her own story, but she spoke for many.*

---

* For more information about REACH in Rwanda, or to contact Gerry Gardner, visit www.reach-rwanda.org and www.reachusa.org.

*Agnes is a Hutu who had married a Tutsi man named John, and together they raised five children. Being Hutu or Tutsi was never an issue for them but simply the acknowledgment of one's societal group, distinctions that dated back to the days when Rwanda was a colony under Belgian rule before 1959. Yet they could not ignore the growing tensions in Rwanda as conflicting views about the country's efforts to become independent began to arise.*

*For years, the government's power had been in the hands of the minority Tutsis, who then fled across the borders to surrounding countries when the Hutu extremist leaders assumed control in 1959. Now in 1994, there was obvious division over the signing of a treaty for shared government. John and Agnes heard the talk in the streets and the arguments at the marketplaces. They felt the unease all around them and were greatly concerned about the hate messages being perpetrated by Radio Rwanda. There were rumors of Hutu militia being trained and caches of clubs and machetes stored in hidden places, but what was one to do but go on with daily life? And pray.*

*Then came news in early April of that year that the Rwandan president's plane had been shot down as he was returning from signing the agreement for a government that would be representative of both Hutus and Tutsis. Agnes was concerned when she heard the news — a concern that quickly turned to confusion and fear as roadblocks were set up throughout Rwanda within hours. These roadblocks were for the sole purpose of keeping the "cockroach Tutsis" in place as the vicious killings began. Agnes heard, as word spread from village to village, that no Tutsi was to be spared, and she immediately sought to find a safe place for her husband, John, to hide.*

*Though Agnes's brothers were Hutus, she trusted them and asked for their help to save her family. Never could Agnes have imagined their response—they killed her husband and then allowed her to be raped by other Hutus in front of four of her children, only then to kill them too. No children of "cockroaches" could be allowed to live. Her home was completely destroyed by her nephews, and all of her belongings were stolen.*

When we are in the middle of a horrific crisis, we often expect our closest family members and friends to give us support and help. So I was horrified to learn what Agnes experienced when she turned to her family for help.

*Lost in grief and suffering, Agnes sought help from her in-laws, bringing them the horrible news of their son's death and that of their grandchildren. Instead of welcome and comfort, they blamed her for the deaths of her family members. Utterly alone and in shock, Agnes wandered the streets, now flowing red with the blood of the genocide victims. Everywhere she looked, Agnes saw death and cried out for God to have mercy. After she was raped again, beaten, and left for dead, mercy finally came when someone took her to a hospital, where she was treated for her physical injuries.*

*Thirteen years after the genocide, Agnes attended a Christian seminar that taught about forgiveness—about how God sent his Son to die in order to reconcile us to himself and to others. Agnes heard how she needed to forgive those who killed her husband and children to truly live as a Christian. She cried uncontrollably as she went home that day in anger, thinking about all that had happened to her.*

*Two months later at a second seminar, Agnes spoke up and described the wretchedness of what she had endured during the genocide. All who listened were in tears. As she finished her story, Agnes said, "I now forgive my brothers, my father-in-law, and my mother-in-law. I forgive those who killed my four children, those who raped me in public in front of my children. I forgive all who stole my belongings and those who destroyed my house. I forgive myself—and may the Lord forgive them and me also. I have come to realize that living with hatred and anger damages me more, and I need to forgive in order to be forgiven. I thank God for helping me through."*

Gerry reports that Agnes now serves as a leader in the REACH organization in Rwanda. Agnes allowed the Lord to restore her peace as the stain of unforgiveness was wiped from her soul. I was stunned to learn that she visits her brothers in prison, taking them meals. She told them she forgave them, even before they said they were sorry for all the suffering they caused her. She has a new home, recently built for her by some of the released genocide prisoners who are making reparation for their crimes. Gerry said, "This home has now allowed Agnes to begin a new family as she takes in orphan children and gives them a place to call their own."

Gerry has witnessed that daily life continues in Rwanda, even though the pain of 1994 can never be forgotten — only forgiven.

*Each time I return to Rwanda, Agnes is there to greet me. She now walks among the widows and the wives of the perpetrators as they gather together to support each other, all victims of one of the darkest moments in human history. She teaches, sings, hugs, comforts, and hands them cloths for their tears. And she models a freedom that can only come from a deep surrender to Christ's love — a love that gives forgiveness to all.*

What my mind struggles to comprehend about unquenchable faith is now perfectly clear through the story of Agnes — one woman who embraced faith in God, even when she was subjected to a firestorm of agony most of us cannot imagine. Her life demonstrates that forgiveness frees us from the burden of living in a prison of our own making. Her visits to her brothers and her care of them after the degrading and horrific pain they thrust on her are living proof that a big part of forgiveness is forgoing our "right" to hurt others for hurting us. Her unquenchable faith does not mean she forgets the genocide or diminishes the severity of the wrongs done to her and to her family. But her stalwart faith, made more invincible by great sorrow, has allowed her to let go of anger, bitterness, and resentment. She is a woman who is free indeed!

You and I can follow in this pathway forged by Agnes. We can embrace a life of faith even when we are in agony, knowing that God will free us from the prison of our own making — our bitterness, our unforgiveness, our resentments, our "what ifs," and our "if onlys." Like Agnes, we will be made more invincible by great sorrow as we lock our eyes on Jesus and follow in his footsteps through life on this earth until we reach our true and final home.

## Our Journey toward Unquenchable Faith

We began our journey through this book together, acknowledging that we all face moments when the fire of our faith wanes and even threatens to go out. We explored how and why our faith-fire can grow weak, and we learned the importance of building a faith that endures. We discovered that when fire-storms come — and they will — God is with us in the fire and will rescue us in his perfect timing. Yet, even if he does not, we know he is the God of the flame, and we can place our complete, eternal confidence in him.

We discovered that the intense heat of a fire creates embers that keep our faith alive until new fuel arrives or until the wind of God's Spirit lifts those embers to a new location to begin a new blaze. We celebrated our burning bush moments and learned how recounting what the Lord has done can sustain us through any wilderness as we realize that wherever we are, we are standing on holy ground.

We explored how to see the spark and be the spark as we play our part in building a wildfire faith in others, and we learned how to tend the fire of our faith by nurturing our relationship with our heavenly Father. God is the God of light, and he is in the business of piercing the darkness. So we committed ourselves to reflecting his light to a hurting and broken world.

The Refiner's fire, though painful, is our invitation to be rid of the impurities and dross that threaten to extinguish our faith and to be refined until we reflect the character and image of our Maker. Every step of the way, we met fellow believers who, like us, are heaven bound.

## Faith That Endures

I hope that you, like me, are committed to growing a wildfire faith that endures all things. As I met the people whose stories are told throughout this book — people who have suffered and have seen few tangible answers to their desperate prayers — I observed their faith under fire, and I grew stronger in my own faith. Their wildfire faith added fuel to my fire and showed me how to focus on the resurrection power that will carry me into the very presence of God for all eternity. The writer of Hebrews perfectly expresses the power of such examples:

> Do you see what this means — all these pioneers who blazed the way, all these veterans cheering us on? It means we'd better get on with it. Strip down, start running — and never quit! No extra spiritual fat, no parasitic sins. Keep your eyes on *Jesus*, who both began and finished this race we're in. Study how he did it. Because he never lost sight of where he was headed — that exhilarating finish in and with God — he could put up with anything along the way: cross, shame, whatever. And now he's *there*, in the place of honor, right alongside God. When you find yourselves flagging in your faith, go over that story again, item by item, that long litany of hostility he plowed through. *That* will shoot adrenaline into your souls!
>
> HEBREWS 12:1 – 3

So let's get on with it, this building of a wildfire faith that will endure anything! Keep your eyes on Jesus and never lose sight of where you are headed. You can put up with anything along the way — shame, persecution, suffering, sacrifice ... anything — because you know where you are headed. God is the source of that first flicker that sparked your faith, and one day you will stand in his holy presence, look into the flaming eyes of Jesus, and see his burning love for you face-to-face.

Until that day, may the wildfire of your faith sustain you through every obstacle and continue to change the landscape of your world as you draw others to the God of the flame.

## COME TO THE FIRE

1. Which of the following statements best describes your faith right now?

❑ My faith is wavering.

❑ My faith is dead.

❑ My faith is strong — as long as I don't experience suffering.

❑ My faith is unquenchable — no matter what I'm going through.

❑ Other:

What events, relationships, or circumstances have impacted the current state of your faith?

2. All of us love to read about the "Hall of Faith" biblical leaders in Hebrews 11, who had miraculous rescues, escapes, and mountain-moving spiritual victories. But then comes the words that are hard to read: "There were those who, under torture, refused to give in and go free, preferring something better" (Hebrews 11:35). The descriptions of their hardships make us cringe. Read Hebrews 12:1 – 3 and record what produced unshakable faith in those individuals.

3. What were the most inspiring and challenging parts of Agnes's story? What part do you think forgiveness played in her ability to move on to healthy choices and to a place of leading a productive life? Lewis Smedes once wrote, "When you release the wrong-doer from the wrong ... you set a prisoner free, but you discover that the real prisoner was yourself." In what ways would you say this statement has been true or not true in your own experience?

4. What has impacted your life in the most powerful way through this book?

## FAITH-BUILDING CHALLENGE

If lack of forgiveness is holding you back from wildfire faith, start by writing out your own definition of forgiveness. Then fill in the blanks here and turn your words into a prayer: *Lord, I need to forgive* _____.
*My emotions of [fear, anger, disappointment, resentment]* _____ *have kept me in a prison of my own making. I confess to you all wrong thinking and wrongdoing on my part, and I ask for your wisdom about what steps to take next that will move me in the direction of restoration, redemption, and unquenchable faith. Amen.*

# Acknowledgments

One of my favorite activities is to brainstorm with Christian leaders about the most effective ways to spread messages of truth, hope, encouragement, perseverance, and joy to people who will ignite wildfire faith in the lives of others.

The catalyst for this book was the input of my longtime friend and extraordinarily gifted editor, Cindy Lambert. She knew I wanted to write about a faith that would outlast my life and that I deeply cared about impacting women who felt like their once-vibrant belief in God's promises was now smoldering amid the crushing heaviness of disappointments or tough circumstances. Cindy also caught my vision and passion for creating a book that would give Christian women tools for sparking a desire in others to develop unquenchable faith.

After two years of praying, thinking, meeting together, and jotting down ideas, Cindy birthed the concept of growing a wildfire faith that would outlast anything. I am in her debt for the idea that became *Unquenchable*. Cindy, your gifts as a vision caster and as a collaborative editor are matched by your compassion for those who are walking through personal firestorms. As this book came together, your heart beat with mine, and I sensed God's Spirit permeating the manuscript with timeless truth. Thank you for making me a better writer by asking the hard questions and by requesting that I go back to the drawing board when necessary. This project has truly been a joint effort!

I am also indebted to my team of intercessors, led by Sandi Banks and Kathy Blume. Your prayer support for Gene and me as we travel in ministry, for Jason as he continues to live and minister behind the razor wire, and for the writing of this manuscript provides fuel that keeps us going. I know the powerful demonstration of God's work in the hearts of audiences and readers is a direct result of your poignant prayer. Thank you!

It is in being real in the telling of our stories that we give other people permission to be open and honest about their own lives. I'm grateful to the friends who shared in this book their experiences and the lessons learned—Jackie Edwards, Lynn Morrissey, Cindy Lambert, "Carrie," Cindee Riordan, Deric Alvis, "Katie," Tanya Glanzman, and Gerry Gardner. Your authenticity inspires me to be appropriately vulnerable so others can grow.

My family has been a major support during the completion of this project. Thank you to my husband, Gene, for his tangible help with household and ministry tasks while I wrote, for supplying me with lots of coffee, for providing humor when I needed a break, and for sharing from his personal journal in one of the chapters. Thanks, also, to my son, Jason, for his honest contribution to this project. A big shout-out goes to my sister, Paula Afman, for her willingness to reveal the pain of her past to give other women an opportunity to know there can be renewed life after firestorms destroy everything except things that last forever. Thanks, too, to my precious mother, Pauline Afman, who reminds me there is always hope when we know Jesus.

Finally, thank you to the gifted publishing team at Zondervan for their outstanding support of this manuscript. Sandra

Vander Zicht, associate publisher and executive editor, championed this book from the beginning and provided "editorial love" to the content editing. Working in tandem with the editorial genius of Sandra Vander Zicht and Cindy Lambert has been a rare privilege. Tom Dean, senior director of marketing, worked with his team to create a cover that grabs my heart and a publicity plan that will allow the greatest number of people to hear about this book. Production editor Dirk Buursma polished the manuscript with tender loving care and excellent craftsmanship. Author Care director Joyce Ondersma continues to meet my needs before I ask for help. I appreciate all of you so much!

Most of all, thank you to my Lord Jesus Christ for giving me a message that burns in my heart, fresh energy to speak and write, a renewed hope for each day, and a joy that endures.

# Notes

Page 20: *True atheists do not:* Philip Yancey, *Disappointment with God* (Grand Rapids: Zondervan, 1992), 41.

Page 25: *My friend Lynn can relate:* Lynn D. Morrissey, author of *Love Letters to God: Deeper Intimacy through Written Prayer,* AWSA speaker, and certified journal facilitator; e-mail: words@brick.net.

Page 32: *Faith means believing in advance:* Philip Yancey, *Where Is God When It Hurts?* (Grand Rapids: Zondervan, 1977, 1990), 161.

Page 34: *Submission to God's sovereignty:* Nancy Guthrie, *Holding On to Hope* (Wheaton, IL: Tyndale House, 2002), 90 – 91.

Page 41: *Such a fire is beyond: Encyclopædia Britannica Online,* "Fire storm," www.britannica.com/EBchecked/topic/207883/fire-storm (accessed July 20, 2013).

Page 57: *They return nutrients to the soil: National Geographic Online,* "Wildfires," http://environment.nationalgeographic.com/environment/natural-disasters/wildfires/ (accessed July 20, 2013).

Page 71: *Embers are the glowing, hot coals:* Reference.com, "ember," www.reference.com/browse/ember?s=t&path=/ (accessed July 20, 2013).

Page 125: *Mom, God is doing something powerful:* Carol Kent, *Between a Rock and a Grace Place* (Grand Rapids: Zondervan, 2010), 153 – 54.

Page 132: *Untended fires soon die:* Gail MacDonald, quoted in *One Holy Passion,* compiled by Judith Couchman (Colorado Springs: WaterBrook, 1998), 29.

Page 147: *I share a story about how my doorbell rang:* Adapted from Carol Kent, *When I Lay My Isaac Down* (Colorado Springs: NavPress, 2004), 75–76.

Page 167: *Restore to me the joy:* Psalm 51:12 NIV.

Page 170: *There is no painless path to heaven:* John Piper, "He Is Like a Refiner's Fire," www.desiringgod.org/resource-library/sermons/he-is-like-a-refiners-fire (accessed July 20, 2013).

Page 180: *The only way to learn:* Quoted in L. B. Cowman, *Streams in the Desert* (Grand Rapids: Zondervan, 1996), 171.

Page 186: *My friend Tanya is facing down:* To contact Tanya Glanzman, go to myfathersdaughter.com or to laughinginthestorm.wordpress.com.

Page 191: *He comes to us in the brokenness:* Robert Farrar Capon, *The Astonished Heart: Reclaiming the Good News from the Lost-and-Found of Church History* (Grand Rapids: Eerdmans, 1996), 15.

Page 198: *Faith is deliberate confidence:* Harry Verploegh, ed., *The Oswald Chambers Devotional Reader* (Nashville: Nelson, 1990), 76.

Page 201: *Well planned by Hutu extremists:* United Human Rights Council, "Genocide in Rwanda," www.unitedhumanrights.org/genocide/genocide_in_rwanda.htm (accessed July 20, 2013).

Page 212: *When you release the wrongdoer:* Lewis Smedes, *Forgive and Forget: Healing the Hurts We Don't Deserve*, 2nd ed. (San Francisco: HarperSanFrancisco, 2007), 133.

# About Carol Kent

Carol Kent is an international public speaker and bestselling author. She is the director of Speak Up Conference, a ministry that equips the next generation to speak, to write, and to lead. She is also the president of Speak Up Speaker Services (a speakers bureau) and the founder of Speak Up for Hope, an organization that ministers to inmates and their families. Carol is an expert on public speaking, on writing, and on encouraging people to hold on to hope when life's circumstances turn out differently from their dreams.

Carol speaks weekly all over the United States and has carried her inspiring messages to South Africa, Germany, Bulgaria, China, Korea, Hong Kong, Guatemala, Mexico, and Canada. She regularly appears on a wide variety of nationally syndicated radio and television broadcasts, and she sits on the advisory boards of MOPS International and the Advanced Writers and Speakers Association. Her articles have been published in a wide variety of magazines, and she is the author of numerous books, including *When I Lay My Isaac Down*, *A New Kind of Normal*, *Between a Rock and a Grace Place*, *Becoming a Woman of Influence*, *Secret Longings of the Heart*, *Tame Your Fears*, and *Speak Up with Confidence*.

Carol's goal is to encourage readers and conference attendees to start a wildfire faith that will lead people to irrepressible hope, restored joy, and vibrant trust in God. In every book and in each presentation, she will share biblical truth delivered with a touch of humor that will lift your spirits and point to eternal Truth. Carol and her husband, Gene, live in Lakeland, Florida.

To book Carol for speaking engagements, call 586-481-7661 or request additional information at www.CarolKent.org.

For information on Speak Up Conference, go to www.SpeakUpConference.com.

To learn more about the nonprofit organization Gene and Carol have launched, go to www.SpeakUpforHope.org.

# Between a Rock and a Grace Place

## Divine Surprises in the Tight Spots of Life

*Carol Kent*, Bestselling Author of *When I Lay My Isaac Down*

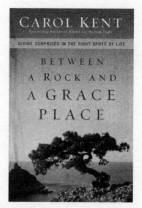

Carol Kent and her husband, Gene, understand heartbreak. Their son, Jason, a young man who initially had so much promise, is now serving a life sentence for murder in a maximum-security prison. All their appeals have been exhausted at both the state and federal levels—humanly speaking, they have run out of options.

Despite their grim situation, Carol and Gene live a life full of grace. Carol reveals how life's problems are a fruitful backdrop for discovering the very best divine surprises, including peace, compassion, freedom, and adventure.

Through their remarkable ongoing journey, Jason's riveting letters from behind bars, and true "grace place" stories from the lives of others, Carol testifies to the reality that when seemingly insurmountable challenges crash into our lives, we can be transformed as we discover God at work in ways we never imagined.

*Available in stores and online!*

**is a nonprofit organization that seeks
to live out the principle of Proverbs 31:8–9:**

*Speak up for the people who have no voice,
for the rights of all the down-and-outers.
Speak out for justice.
Stand up for the poor and destitute!*

**Vision:** To help inmates and their families adjust to their *new normal*.

**Mission:** We exist to provide hope to inmates and their families through encouragement and resources.

It is the goal of Speak Up for Hope to give hope to the hopeless, encouragement and strength to the weary, reparation to marriages that have been torn apart by incarceration, and mental, spiritual, and physical stability to the children of prisoners.

We pray that people all over the world will begin speaking up for those who cannot speak up for themselves. As people become the hands and feet of Jesus to "the least of these," something miraculous happens. As we choose to get personally involved by giving, volunteering, and praying, we are transformed from the inside out as we model for others how to become hope givers.

Gene, Carol, and Jason Kent

For more information on the variety of ways
in which you can be involved
in Speak Up for Hope, please contact:

**Speak Up for Hope**
P.O. Box 6262
Lakeland, FL 33807-6262
www.SpeakUpforHope.org
888.987.1212

Make tax-deductible contributions payable to
Speak Up for Hope,
or donations can be made online at
www.SpeakUpforHope.org.

## Share Your Thoughts

**With the Author:** Your comments will be forwarded to the author when you send them to *zauthor@zondervan.com*.

**With Zondervan:** Submit your review of this book by writing to *zreview@zondervan.com*.

## Free Online Resources at
## www.zondervan.com

**Daily Bible Verses and Devotions:** Enrich your life with daily Bible verses or devotions that help you start every morning focused on God. Visit www.zondervan.com/newsletters.

**Free Email Publications:** Sign up for newsletters on Christian living, academic resources, church ministry, fiction, children's resources, and more. Visit www.zondervan.com/newsletters.

**Zondervan Bible Search:** Find and compare Bible passages in a variety of translations at www.zondervanbiblesearch.com.

**Other Benefits:** Register to receive online benefits like coupons and special offers, or to participate in research.